MW01492209

Ending White Slavery

by

Matthew Hale

Copyright © 2015
Matthew Hale
All rights reserved
ISBN13: 9781514246184
ISBN10: 151424618X

front cover: Montage © 2015 Georgio Unchino
back cover: Declaration of Independence John Trumbull

Chapter One
Our Minds Are In Chains

I write these words from a prison cell but it is the minds of our White people that are in chains. To serve as a means by which those chains may be broken would be the highest calling of which I know; to succeed would be the greatest victory. The chains of the body are easily broken—all one needs is a hammer and a chisel, after all—but chains of the mind? Such chains are of much harder stuff and yet are not so visible to our eyes. Where do we strike? And how do we do so without wounding ourselves? For the links are more tightly forged than those upon any chained body.

The minds of our White people are in chains...but can we even utter the words "White people," today? Have not the chains upon our minds become so tight, so fixed, that the very notion of a "White people" has become anathema to us? Are we not in fact imbued with the idea that we shouldn't even utter or contemplate such words, that there are Whites, yes, and there are people, yes, but "White people," together? Such a notion as "White people" is a mistake, a misfortune, a moral failing, we have been told. We are not supposed to have an identity as White people; rather, we are supposed to be individuals who just happen to be White. When asked our race, we are almost apologetic with our answer as if to say, "yes, I'm a White guy, one of those insignificant White males perhaps, but hey, I couldn't help it...but I wish I could!" What a sickness to behold, a sickness of the mind. I wish it were untrue—I would dream that it were so—but true it is: *a people is today unwilling to believe that it even exists.* It would rather think its existence away, to wish it away, to banish from its hearts and minds its very name. Such would be pleasing to it. The minds of our White people are indeed in chains.

And they are chains of our own making, chains of our own fabrication! It is we who have placed our minds within the chains of the slave or allowed it to be so placed. It is we who have forfeited our own freedom of thought as a people in obeisance to what we have assumed to be the needs and desires of others. It is we who in the name of freedom have actually forsaken it where it matters most. It is we who have placed our minds in manacles every bit as thick and restraining as those to be found anywhere. In fact, we have truly become less free than the slave in the field. Yes, the slave in the field must work, performing a labor not of his own choosing, but at least his thoughts were free and he did not forget his identity as part of the race to which he belonged. We though, as White people, today stand as pariahs within our own skins, guilty of crimes uncommitted, and as foreigners within our own country. We are today's outcasts unwilling to speak for fear of giving offense, with tongues unable to form even the syllables of a truly free people, and syllables unable to form the words of pride, respect, honor, and love directed upon that people, White people, much less feel it and show it.

You think I exaggerate? Then let me ask you this: would you feel comfortable donning a T-shirt in public that says "I'm proud to be White" upon it? If you are a political leader, would you be comfortable stating on camera that you are concerned about the future of *White* people? If you are a wealthy businessman, would you be willing to publicly announce an endowment to create a United *White* College Fund? If you are a "community organizer," as our current president was, would you be willing to openly organize Whites *as Whites*?

If you are a college student, do you feel free to create a White Student Alliance alongside the Black, Latino, and Asian? Do you feel free to open your mouth in class to defend the so-called "dead white males" as they are being castigated by your professor? Do you feel free to proclaim to the world that you are proud to be White and see no reason to apologize for anything your ancestors supposedly "did" to the other races? If not, you are indeed in chains, your actions fettered by the enslaved minds of others—or by the chains that grip your own mind.

Even the word "race" is distasteful to you, is it not? It is a word encased with fear and dread, a word that you would rather not have exist, that should not be uttered in polite company, that should be swept away under a rug someplace but alas, my brethren, such sentiments are only held by *White* people! Not the black, not the brown, and not the yellow. They do not run when the word is uttered, so why should you? They are not bashful about it, so why should you be? Why must you be half a man and they full? Why must your chin be low and theirs high? You have become so accustomed to the double standard that it is ingrained in your soul and you forget that it even exists.

What is acceptable for the others is not acceptable for you. What is open to the others is not open to you. What the others would want, you think yourself to have no right to want. This is the depth of your degradation, that you would think yourself to be entitled to so little and must forsake so much for the benefit of the others, that you must always accommodate rather than be the one accommodated. What chains have been forged upon the minds of our people that we would think it just to forbear ourselves at every turn!

Much has become habit for you but to be habitual is not to be right. You have become habituated to thinking and acting in certain ways, but what if these ways are wrong? You wish to be fair but should your fairness not also include being fair to yourself, and if it is right to be fair to yourself, should you not also be fair to your own people from whom you sprang? Does your people, yes, White people as *White people*, deserve not at least some kind of consideration, some kind of regard in this world? Is it wrong to think about ourselves, to care about ourselves, to want a future for ourselves, and if we do not, who will? Is it wrong to claim an existence for ourselves that we would deign not to be besmirched, a future for ourselves that we would prefer not to be doubtful, a present for ourselves that we would not like to see humiliated?

Must we always grovel before our mistreatment, always bow before any accusation, always assume that we as a people, and yes *we as a race*, are always in the wrong?

It is legal for the government of the United States to discriminate in favor of the black, brown, and yellow and yet illegal for it to do so in favor of the White. "Affirmative Action" they call the first; "racism" they call the second. The insane are indeed never conscious of their insanity, are they? The double-standard is swallowed as "justice"; the pain of White people is disregarded as "progress," but it is a "justice" and "progress" never for *you,* is it, White man? You have been written out of such fine words. They are not to be applied to you.

"Civil rights" are likewise only civil rights for the brown, black, and yellow in this society in which we live. If you doubt that, I ask you, have you ever heard of anybody in power discuss "the civil rights of White people"? In any shape or form? "Civil rights" are simply something alien to White people and if you picture a "civil rights leader" in your mind, your image will automatically assume the configuration of a black or a brown person. Yes, you will hear talk of White civil rights workers but it is the "civil rights" of *non-*whites for which it is understood that they work. The idea that there could be actual civil rights of *White* people at stake, in any manner, simply never enters our people's minds. Show up at the Equal Employment and Opportunity Commission and announce that you wish to work for the equal rights of White people and watch yourself be laughed at and shown the door. White people are simply not on the agenda for White people have been defined out of the very idea of "civil rights" just as they have been defined out of the very idea of progress and justice. There is no "progress," "justice," or "civil rights" for White people in their dealings with non-white people; these terms, and indeed these ideals, are reserved for the non-whites only. "Equality" can be talked about until people are blue in the face but the "equality" that people have in mind is only for those who are *not* White. If you are concerned about "civil rights," the rights in question are automatically that of *non*-whites. You, as a White man, can go to work for the "civil rights" of the brown, the black, and the yellow only, for White people have no "civil rights" that exist or need be respected. The definition of "civil rights" doesn't include anything having to do with White people as a people except for when they are the *servants* of others. The minds of our White people are indeed in chains.

It is absolutely expected that White people will dig deep into their pockets and spend their time and energy to further the "civil rights" of the black man by supporting the National Association for the Advancement of Colored People (NAACP) and the United Negro College Fund but who would imagine, let alone expect, black people supporting a National Association for the Advancement of *White* People and a United *White* College Fund? The very idea illuminates the absurdity of our White people of today. White people who support a White movement and a college fund for White students are labeled by the mass media as "the fringe" for simply trying to do for their own people what, amazingly, their own White people are *expected* to do *for the others* who would never reciprocate and for which the very idea *no one would ever imagine.* Thus in our sick society, to care about the future of "colored people" is a "crusade for civil rights" but to care about the future of White people is "racism," "bigotry," and "hatred." Blacks can unambiguously assert a black agenda and be applauded by the media and the government, but unambiguously asserting a White agenda, oh my goodness, what a fiend you are! With the minds of our people in such chains, chains on the body are unnecessary, are they not?

Whenever there is a supposed forum on race, the entire event is devoted to whether *blacks* are treated well enough to meet *their* satisfaction, whether White people have yet successfully "atoned" for their supposed sins, and what else White people can do to please blacks even further. The happiness and satisfaction of White people are never part of the "forum" at all. We are not supposed to care about such things, let alone discuss them. The media commentators joyfully proclaim that here, on their show, "both sides" are presented on the question of "Race in America" but these "sides" are merely composed of non-whites, and those Whites whose entire mindset is devoted exclusively to the appeasement of non-whites and to the utter disregard of White people as White people with rightful interests of their own.

If a White member of the audience were to have the temerity to ask the panel of so-called "experts," "What about the best interests of White people?," he would either be shouted down, interrupted, a convenient commercial break would be taken, or the "experts" would quickly respond by saying that they (supposedly) care about the best interests of "all people"...but that White people have a "special responsibility" to redress the 'horrible discrimination' that they have meted out to black people over the years. In other words, again, White people have no independent existence of their own; their race is only to be considered in relation to whether they have collectively redressed their alleged sins and made blacks sufficiently contented and smug. We are to be 100 percent "sensitive" to the feelings and wants of the black man and 0 percent sensitive to the feelings and wants of the White. This is further illustrated by numerous "sensitivity training courses" that have sprouted up across the land (like poisonous mushrooms?). Does anyone really think that the sensitivity in question is in regards to the feelings of *White* people, in any shape, manner, or form?

The minds of our White people are in chains. We don't even think twice about referring to "white trash" on national television but who among those people saying that would comfortably use the words "*black* trash" in the same venue? Our minds and our society are so sick that the vast majority of people do not view the first as racist language and yet indeed *would* view the second that way. Have not the minds of our people become perverted when we can feel perfectly entitled to call our own White people "trash" but think that the heavens may fall if we call *another* people "trash"? Why though would we deny our own people the respect that we bestow to others? Why is it that we are willing to besmirch our own people at the drop of a hat and yet fear that the heavens may fall if we were to be critical of the black, brown, and yellow? What kind of "equality" is this? Indeed, the preachers of "equality" have, in actuality, rendered White people *inferior* within their own minds. It is an inferiority that they would like to maintain. The schools teach it, the government requires it, and the media reinforce it. When still a child, the mind of the White person has already been placed in chains through the entire fabric of the debasing society in which he lives.

How else can one explain the controversy that ensued when a White United States Senator was quoted as using the word "Negro" in a private conversation—as if this were somehow an offensive term—when there exists a United *Negro* College Fund that collects millions of dollars every year without objection, mostly from White people? (There were demands for his apology and even calls for his resignation when the man had simply been praising then presidential candidate Barack Obama, using a term that had historically been one of *respect*!) When a people is not even free to use the words that naturally come to it, how can it be considered free? Thus the Negroes can call themselves Negroes but when a White man does so in a moment of *praise*, a controversy ensues for days on end all over the television set and in the newspapers. White people have lost the right to even determine what is offensive and what is not; instead, it is up to the "Negro" to decide. Nor do the apologies of White people extend only to actual wrongdoing anymore; rather, they are wrung out of us at will and one apology is never enough. Have you noticed that it is always the *White* people who do the apologizing, that they are never the ones apologized to? That it is only the *White* people who grovel, never the non-whites? White people are expected to walk tip toe on pins and needles but when non-whites stomp their feet, we do not hesitate to pronounce them justified. When they claim to be outraged, they are always deemed to be in the right. On the other hand, is it not true that we as White people have been stripped of our very right of outrage at anything that non-whites do, in any manner? Occasionally our tongues will slip the harness imposed upon ourselves but we always know that a harness is there. True, we are responsible for the harness ourselves but we are no less slaves for it. The minds of our people are in chains.

The way those in power would have it, the only discrimination that occurs in America is by Whites against non-whites, that the only so-called "hate crimes" involving race that occur in America are that of Whites against non-whites, that the only slavery that has occurred has been that of Whites enslaving blacks, and that whenever blacks are behind Whites in any respect "socio-economically," this must assuredly be a "vestige of slavery and Jim Crow laws" (i.e. the fault of the White man too). Alas, my brethren, the reality is that the vast majority of racial discrimination that occurs in America is *against* Whites through legalized discrimination (so-called affirmative action), that the vast majority of racial hate crimes consist of non-white perpetrators and White victims, that slavery has been practiced throughout history all over the world and owes its very name to the enslavement of *White* people (the Slavs of Eastern Europe), and that blacks are also behind White people socio-economically in places where they were *never* subjected to slavery or Jim Crow laws by Whites and thus their lag would have existed had White people been nowhere to be found. The "debt" that we are alleged to owe is simply not owed at all and nor is there any guilt on our part for which there should be repentance. The whole foundation though of anything having to do with race in this society is White guilt, White penance, and White resignation. We are supposed to feel guilty for blacks having been enslaved in America but where is the responsibility of blacks for having enslaved one another in Africa for thousands of years before a single White man ever owned a slave? Where is the responsibility of blacks for having sold fellow blacks into slavery to Whites in the first place? And why should the very few actual White slaveholders of blacks impugn the entire White people of today anyway? My ancestors did not own black slaves and yours probably didn't either, but even if they did, how can it be morally right to cast stones upon those who gave us life in *any* dispute concerning another people? In other words, how can we morally justify defaming the memory of our own ancestors in favor of the present sentiments of another race? Instead, we should side with our own people, our own ancestors, rather than betray them to the wolves. To be sure, the current generation does not have a monopoly on morality and if our ancestors did things which we may find perplexing today, this does not mean that we would not have done the same thing had we been in their shoes. In any case, where is the justice in blaming the children for the deeds not of the parents, not of the grandparents, but rather of the great-great-grandparents and beyond?

We are not supposed to hold our heads high as White people but rather be White people in spite of ourselves. We are not supposed to celebrate our ancestors but rather be ashamed of them if they were Southerners (for Negro slavery), Northerners (for conquering the Indians), or simply Europeans (for persecuting Jews). If we are Australians, we are discounted as being descended from criminals; if we are South Africans we are claimed to be thieves of black lands; if we are Italians we are painted as Mafioso; and if we are Germans we are smeared as warmongers. When we reflect upon the conquest of the American west, we are supposed to take the side of the Indians *over that of our own people.* (Indeed, we are not supposed to consider them "Indians" at all any longer but rather as "Native," or 'true' Americans, with us presumably being the false ones!) When we reflect upon the American Civil War, the ending of Negro slavery is claimed to be more important than the deaths of over 600,000 White men. When we reflect upon the Second World War, it is "The Holocaust" that is remembered rather than the deaths of tens of millions of non-Jewish White men, women, and children. Our White people are simply not as important as the Indians, Negroes, and Jews. White men can be scalped, bled to death on a battlefield, or burned alive in the fire-bombing of civilians but their lives are simply not as important. This is the horrific message that is indeed sent to the world and with which our people are imbued. This is the message that has bored its way deep within our psyche: *we are the bad guys.* Those who are *not* White are the good, the oppressed, the healthy, the innocent; those who *are* White are the evil, the oppressors, the sick, the guilty. Slavery was supposedly "America's original sin" and who participated in it? White people, and therefore they are guilty, *all of them.* No one ever bothers to even prove that this or that White man actually had an ancestor who was a slave owner; rather, all White men are simply guilty for being White and must "atone" for their supposed guilt, not as individuals but as an entire race. (Isn't it telling that in positive matters, it is demanded that we be mere "individuals" but when it comes to our alleged guilt only, we are instead held to be a *race*? How quaint!) Even if your ancestors or mine didn't come to America until *after* the Civil War, it is to no avail. You share the same gene pool, White man, and must therefore tolerate legalized discrimination against you ("affirmative action"), Negro college funds but no White college funds, and a host of other indicia of second class citizenship. More importantly though, you must suffer a perpetual feeling of guilt that can never be assuaged.

The matter though goes even deeper. If you have a pale complexion, you are ridiculed and considered sickly and are not considered right until you have darkened yourself upon a beach or under an artificial tanning bed. Your Whiteness is called a blemish, deemed a deficiency, a blight, even an abnormality. You are defective, White man; that too is the message that is sent and it has been duly received and imbibed. Darken your skin! Be ashamed of what you are! Don't you wish that you weren't White? Aren't you unlucky to be so fair?

Was it not once the case though that to be fair was considered a great blessing? "A fair maiden," after all. The lighter the complexion, the more beautiful one was considered, the more noble, the more desirous. There is no tale of old from our history extolling "the dark maiden." Rather, only with White debasement has milky skin become a curse, a well-nigh perversion. In every so-called "Miss America" pageant today, for example, every single White contestant sports an artificial, sometimes chemically-induced tan with *not one* willing to display a natural White, fair skin. Even if this were the only example of a lack of White self-esteem, it would be enough. Contrast this with the news footage of Miss America pageants of old. What has changed is the thinking of our people with the notion of what is beautiful and what is ugly being reversed. What is White suffers from low esteem; what is dark draws high esteem. The fact is inescapable. White skin is quite simply the object of disdain needing "fixed" as soon as possible and the White Miss America contestants make sure that it is indeed fixed in time for every pageant, some of them undoubtedly for fear that they may lose should they sport their natural, White skin! Since the judges share the collective anti-white psychosis, their fears are indeed sensible. The fact is inescapable that White skin is viewed as being a liability, is it not? Why else would every single White contestant come into the pageant every single year sporting a deep tan? And who really believes that their tans were merely caused by inadvertent exposure to the sun? We have become herd animals reveling in our fakery, our supposed ideal of (tanned) beauty actually being a shame for ourselves as we really are. We have come to disdain what we naturally are and seek to escape it. The minds of our people are indeed in chains.

One would wish that White self-loathing in the physical realm would be sufficiently assuaged by the almost frenzied drive by many of our White people to darken their skin but alas, this is not so. It is also reflected in the drive, though far less prevalent, to inflate our lips with various chemicals in an effort to achieve a non-white appearance. While the saying that someone has "nigger lips" used to be a statement of derision, we must consider the stark fact that White women are now going to doctors by the many thousands in order to procure such lips. Once again, we are met here with a deep-seated feeling that to be White is to be ugly, that to have the natural features of a White woman is to be ugly and to assume the features of a non-white, in particular a Negro, is to acquire beauty. Racial renunciation is thus once again at work. The numbers of women who actually participate in this "lip enhancement" procedure can only be greatly exceeded by the number of women who would also partake in it if the procedure were not painful, relatively expensive, and, to some people thankfully still, considered slightly idiotic.

In fairness though it deserves to be pointed out that in the physical realm, our White people are not alone in their racial self-loathing. The example here is the widespread practice of blacks, especially female blacks, to straighten their hair so as to look more like Whites and even blacks who have a keener sense of pride and love for their own people than the norm engage in this practice, such as alleged "civil rights" activist Al Sharpton. How though can any man (or woman) who is really proud to be black be willing to straighten his hair in order to look more like Whites? Do these millions of blacks never even contemplate the inherent contradiction involved? To be sure, they undoubtedly do it because they think that it makes them look better rather than retaining their kinky, wooly natural hair, but why would they think that having straight (or wavy) hair makes them look better unless they had already formed within their psyche the opinion that the hair of Whites is better than that of blacks? In other words, to assume the physical characteristics of *another* race is to lack esteem for your *own* race. To be black and to straighten one's hair—as to be White and to zealously seek a darker skin and fat lips—is to replace one's own race's ideal of beauty with that of another race, both revealing a lack of esteem for and comfort in what one actually is. You may be tempted to say, "maybe these people just like the black or White look better" but this just begs the question as to why they would like the black or White look better in the first place. No color, or thickness of lips, or texture of hair, after all, has intrinsic superiority in itself but rather has only that superiority which we attach to it, and thus we must naturally ask ourselves what is causing millions of individuals in the various races to reject their own racial traits in pursuit of that of other races. The answer is the presence of a feeling of inferiority as to what they naturally and actually are. White people have become uncomfortable in their own skin (and in some cases, with their own lips!) and in times past there is simply no record of such a perverse phenomenon. White skin, formerly a symbol of beauty, has become, somehow, something to be ashamed of. The complimentary adjective of ivory has been replaced with the pejorative of "pasty." The minds of our White people are in chains.

Of course, it is not a matter of disdaining the exposure of our skin to the pleasant rays of the sun of which we are speaking but rather the almost maniacal frenzy with which so many millions of our White people seek the darkening of their skin out of a sense of disdain for its lighter hue. The former is natural; the latter is a sickness and so is the usage of chemicals to facilitate it. One cannot imagine such a frenzy one hundred years ago when our White people still possessed a sense of self, a sense of self-respect, and self-love as a people. Our ideal of beauty was that of our own kind and there was absolutely no impetus within us to emulate any other people. No matter how White our individual skin, we were content that it stay that way or let it be tanned as it might with the seasons rather than as a matter of any conscious choice. The reversal of this situation, on the other hand, has prompted Nature to respond in a way that was unexpected: go out of your way to seek the darkening of your skin and cancer may be your penalty. Thus Nature herself seems to be telling us to be whom we actually are: White people, not brown or black. It is not, after all, some kind of coincidence that White people today suffer from skin cancer more than the other races by far, for it is our White people who are the only ones in pursuit of "the perfect tan" and this trying to be whom we are not prompts the skin to rebel. What seems obvious is that few of our brethren realize this fact. They are genuinely shocked when they are diagnosed with cancer and feel that they have somehow been aggrieved by their bodies when in reality it is their bodies that are the victims due to a distorted mental state.

The current Miss America pageant notwithstanding, there is nothing more wrong with being fair of skin than being blonde of hair. They of course go together far more than the present myth extolled of fair hair and bronze skin! What though of the situation in which there exists a Miss America pageant in which individuals of all races can and do participate (and win) but there also exists a Miss *Black* America pageant in which only blacks are allowed to participate? There is also, for that matter, a Miss "Latina" pageant in which only hispanics are allowed to participate. This of course begs the question, where is the Miss White America pageant? Is it not a fact that were such a pageant to form that it would be immediately denounced as "racist"? Would not many of our own White people take the lead in the denouncing, perhaps even yourself? How though could such a pageant for only White people be "racist" and the others that are exclusively for the other races not be? Why are we White people cowered into forsaking what the other races are freely allowed to enjoy without fanfare or controversy? There is simply no doubt but that if a Miss White America pageant were to form, the black (of course!) "civil rights" leaders would spring from the woodwork immediately to denounce such a pageant as "discriminatory" and "insensitive" and attack the very name as "racist." How though could a Miss White America pageant be discriminatory and insensitive while Miss Black America and Miss Latina pageants not be, and why is the former any more racist than the latter? Of course, our White people are so cowed, so unassertive, that we would rather not form a pageant for our own people at all than risk the ire of the so-called "civil rights activist" who has practically become some kind of demi-god in society and whose words are to us like pins to hapless butterflies in an insect collection. Whereas we could easily take them to task for the obvious hypocrisy, double-standard, and downright arrogance in their presuming to have any say at all in what White people do, the sick and misplaced guilt in our conscience forbears us here like it does everywhere else in asserting ourselves as a people with an independent existence *and will* of our own. Even the word "insensitive" is indicative of the pansy-like existence that has befallen us: when, in the history of the world, has a race purporting to be manly ever cared about whether its words might be "insensitive" to the feelings of others? When has a race ever sacrificed its own will, its own actions, and even its own attitudes because another race might be discomforted by them? Never until today! Never until today has "sensitivity" been deemed an acceptable substitute for strength, for courage, and even for honor!

So consider the bizarre scenario we have today whereby there exists a Miss Black America pageant (no Whites), a Miss Latina pageant (no Whites), and Miss America pageant where White people participate, all right, but they do their best *not* to look White!

There can be no doubt though that the "civil rights activist" does sincerely take offense at the prospect of a Miss White America pageant, for he *hates* the very words "White America" in themselves. This is an America that he does not want to exist. By attacking the very conception of a "White America," either directly or indirectly, he knows that he will be able to garner special rights and favoritism for his own race (usually black) indefinitely. If there is really a "White America," after all, somebody might get the idea of asserting the *best interests* of White America and all of the special rights and favoritism garnered by the non-whites in our society might be unceremoniously thrown out the window. So, keep White people on the defensive! Attack any and all hints of racial pride in White people and their feeling of any self-worth. Keep them thinking that they owe us (non-whites) for something. Keep White people thinking that they are merely "individuals" rather than a people that might actually exist for themselves like we (non-whites) do. Keep them full of guilt concerning all of the wrongs they supposedly have done. Keep White people as groveling, simpering fools!

This may seem harsh but is this not the reality of the situation?

Is it not the case that the rights of our White people always seem to end wherever and whenever the non-whites assert that theirs begin? Thus the blacks can have their own television channel on the airwaves ("Black Entertainment Television" or "BET") but if some Whites got together and tried to form a White Entertainment Network, they would be accused of "discrimination," "racism," and it is doubtful that a license from the Federal Communications Commission (FCC) would even be forthcoming. Thus the hispanics (mestizoes) can have their own organization devoted to their best interests called "The National Council of La Raza" ("The Race") without the accusation of racism being hurled at it but if some Whites got together and formed a parallel organization called "The White Race," or any other name for that matter, cries of "racism" would, and do, fly. Thus White people can be legally fired for being White but non-whites cannot be legally fired for being non-white. Thus blacks reserve the right to retain "historically black colleges" but historically *White* colleges are banned as "unconstitutional." Thus blacks are allowed to segregate themselves from Whites in the public schools when they deem it in their best interests but Whites are manifestly *not* allowed to do the same when they deem it in *theirs.* Thus blacks and hispanics are given extra "points" in the military and in college entrance exams so that they may be promoted over Whites but a similar practice for the benefit of Whites over blacks and hispanics would be chastised into oblivion.

White people cannot sell their homes to whom they want, cannot rent their apartments to whom they want, cannot allow into their businesses whom they want, and cannot even do business itself with whom they want.

Someone might have the gumption to reply, "Well, of course they can't discriminate on the grounds of race!" Why on earth not? Why should non-whites have a greater right to buy a particular home than the White owner has a right to sell it? Why should non-whites have a greater right to rent a particular apartment than the White owner has a right to rent it out? Why should non-whites have a greater right to use a particular property than the White owner who owns the property? Why should non-whites have a greater right to do business with me than I have a right not to do business with them? And "discrimination"? We as White people are discriminated against all the time both privately and publicly and there are innumerable organizations avowedly for the purpose of advancing non-whites, and non-whites only, and this is discrimination just as surely as the White home or apartment owner who won't sell or rent to blacks, browns, or whomever. All "discrimination" is the favoring of one group of people or things over that of another group of people or things and this happens all the time, *just not for Whites.*

Surely no one is naive enough to think that the millions, or maybe even billions, of dollars that are taken (thieved) from taxpayers each year from their "own" government and given away in the form of "grants" to non-white advocacy groups are also given to White advocacy groups? Surely no one is naive enough to think that the United Negro College Fund gives money to deserving *White* students in order that they may go to college? Surely no one is naive enough to think that the Congressional Black Caucus caucuses for the best interests of White citizens? Who in power, exactly, really looks out for us? No, we are second class citizens and are expected to swallow it and even be grateful for it. As in the movie "Animal House," we are expected to say "Thank you sir, may I please have another?" while we are walloped on the rump in perpetuity.

Oh, I know, the apologists for blacks, browns, and others to look out for their own best interests, for the government to favor them, and for White people to even despise themselves claim that it is so that we can (allegedly) "remedy past inequalities" and (somehow) "make things equal" but why should this be assumed to be a laudable policy goal in the first place? Where does this "equality" business get its halo? Why should we White people forfeit our own best interests just so that the others may allegedly become "equal" to us in their own lives? Why should we tolerate our own mistreatment so that non-whites (especially blacks) may somehow become "equal" to us? Where was it ever written that non-whites even *deserved* "equality" with White people wherever White people happen to live? And how on earth does the mistreatment of the present generation and future ones make up for the supposed wrongs of the past?

If millions of White Frenchmen were to enter China, would the yellow Chinese really be obligated to treat them as equals? Why should they? Why shouldn't they instead prefer their fellow Chinese which is, in other words, an unequal relationship? China is, after all, a yellow country; why should it change its character, its traditions, and its governmental policies to conform to the desires, wishes, and whims of those who are not Chinese? Would it really be sensible for China to cater to the non-Chinese? Would it not be foolish to do so?

By the same token, if millions of Whites were to enter Nigeria, the black Nigerians would be under no obligation to treat them as equals, instead keeping their fellow black Nigerians in a preferential status. White people would have no grounds for complaint in China and nor would they in Nigeria. This "equality" business is a man-made mirage, motes of a sunbeam for which people wildly grope as if they were diamonds without even stopping to consider whether the diamonds (motes) really have any weight. "Equality" seems to be its own justification, its own reward, even though our White people are not, of course, treated equally. We are supposed to hosanna it, bless it without question, practically even pray to it, for "equality" is the false idol of our time. The minds of our White people are indeed in chains, are they not?

While China and Nigeria would not allow millions of White people to enter their borders, and sensibly so, we White people are told we have to open every border we have and if we don't, we are "racists." Thus America is flooded with millions of brown Mexicans pouring across our borders and if we dare to try to deport them, or even have the temerity to pass laws with the intent of identifying them, we are told that we are violating their "rights." How on earth though do people who enter our country illegally (invade) have any rights? Why, as with every other issue involving race, do these invaders have more "rights" to stay here than we who are citizens have the right to determine (or track) who comes into our country? Again, why is it that the rights of White people always seem to end whenever and wherever the non-whites assert that theirs begin?

It is not some kind of remarkable coincidence that all of the hispanic organizations in the United States, "La Raza" and the others, want as many of their brown blood brothers here as possible, supporting the euphemistically-called "undocumented workers" in every way. They do not do so out of the goodness of their hearts, because they are charitable, or because they genuinely believe that such immigration is good for the country as a whole. Rather, they are *brown racists,* quite simply. After all, if millions of White people were invading the United States, can there be any doubt that there would be no hispanic organizations advocating on *their* behalf? In other words, it is the *race* of the brown invaders that motivates these hispanic organizations to advocate for them and nothing else! These brown racists simply want power for their "raza" and they realize, quite rightly, that the more hispanics there are in the U.S., the more power it will have. They want this power not so that they can "share" with White people, or be "equal" with White people, but rather so that they can dominate the society in which they live, White people and everyone else for that matter. And with the minds of our White people in chains, their task is rendered all the easier, for it is *White people themselves* who have tolerated, and indeed legislated, the rapid demographic change of what was once their own country.

Their own country? Yes. In 1950, 85-90 percent of the American population was White and up until that point, the entire world viewed America as a White country and justifiably so considering that White people formed an overwhelming majority. When people thought of a "red-blooded American boy," the image in their minds was that of a *White* boy, not a brown, black, or yellow one. Yes, we had a black minority but this was the only minority of any numerical significance and nobody thought the desires of the 10 to 15 percent racial minority in the country should take precedence over the 85 to 90 percent White majority. Today though, only sixty years later, only 60 percent, if that, of the American population is White. This may well be the fastest demographic change without war in all history. The federal government in Washington, D.C.—which doesn't care at all about White people as White people—wants us to think that this demographic change was somehow inevitable but this is far from the truth. In reality, through its policies, the federal government has deliberately destroyed the White character of our country, replacing it with a mixed character that it did not previously have. In reality, legal immigration is rigged in favor of non-white countries (and has been since legislation was passed in the 1960s) and illegal non-white immigration (invasion) is tolerated by the same government as a means of increasing the cheap labor pool on behalf of big business donors and to appease the hispanic voters who are already here in order to obtain their votes. The votes of White people, though, are never even considered, much less talked about by these politicians because White people are considered to be totally divided, totally individualized, and hence totally neutralized as any kind of racial and interest group block. The politicians thus figure, quite correctly so for the time being, that White people will vote for them no matter *what* they do against the best interests of White America because unlike hispanics, and blacks to an even greater extent, White people simply do not vote as a racial group but rather as willy-nilly "individuals." The politicians consider White people to be too befuddled to know or care that their best interests are being totally disregarded and they are sadly right, for the minds of our White people are in chains. The politicians have betrayed us, have given our country away, have sold out our country for the non-white vote of the moment instead of caring about the welfare of their own people now and in the future.

How often have we heard again and again from news commentators, for example, that the Republican Party risks "backlash" from so-called "Latino" voters if it dares to push a strong immigration policy, as if the "Latino" voters were the only ones who count or even exist? What, though, about backlash from *White* voters? The subject never even comes up, does it? It doesn't come up because, for all practical political purposes, White people don't exist! Our White people are so emasculated indeed that there is not a single White man in political office anywhere today who is willing to state publicly that there are enough non-whites in America as it is, even though as White people we have seen our share of the population in this country drop 25 percent to 30 percent or more in only two generations. Our White people are so emasculated that the only backlash anyone can expect from us has all of the force of a feather. Indeed, we are not even supposed to *think* in terms of "White backlash" for that would involve an assertive

White people, a resolved White people, a united White people, a White people that is free from the mental and physical shackles of guilt and repentance; in other words, a White people that is no longer in chains.

We are also supposed to forget that our White Race was ever the overwhelming majority in this country in the first place and instead think that we were always and inevitably a racially polyglot society. How quaint a lie to imbue the people with by those who betrayed them! There was a time when no one, anywhere, questioned the fact that this was a White country but now, amazingly, nobody remembers that it ever was! How is that for an Orwellian memory hole? "1984" is indeed here.

There are today allegedly forty-five million brown hispanics in the United States. They are considered with a great deal of interest and concern, especially when they do not happen to like the various attempts and hopes of others to control the hispanic illegal immigration (invasion) problem. Right now, at the time of this writing, thousands of them are rallying across the country in protest of a new law in Arizona that merely requires that people there, when already stopped by police for a suspected offense, show proof of legal residence in the U.S. when asked by law enforcement to do so upon reasonable suspicion that the individual is here illegally. They don't like this law and think that that alone means that the law must be repealed. In other words, as far as they are concerned, the people of Arizona, of whatever race, are not entitled to make their own laws. The law must therefore bow before the indignant hispanic (mestizo) who doesn't want to suffer the inconvenience of merely leaving his house with a form of identification confirming that he is in the country legally; this is simply too much for the "gringo" White man to ask! Thus they rally and otherwise protest by the many thousands and *as a race*! White people, who never rally and otherwise protest as a race, witness this and assume that since *they* never rally or protest, that the hispanics must really have a legitimate grievance; that they surely wouldn't be out in the streets if there weren't a just cause for it, would they? Hence White people immediately assume a posture of being on the defense, of placation, of appeasement. "How can we end this controversy?" they ask themselves. Thus they set about to undermine their own laws, laws that their own people just passed, and even rebuke their own people for passing them. Majority rule, needless to say, goes right out the window. Who cares about the majority when the hispanics are upset? No, no, no. It's not majority rule that matters in such an instance but rather, "minority rights"! The minority indeed calls the shots when the majority is confused, deluded, guilt-ridden, and hence divided and at odds with itself. If the rallies and protests aren't enough to cause the law to be repealed, White judges will strike it down. The minority feels aggrieved so the law must go! The grievance that the majority felt in the first place leading to the passage of the law? That is either forgotten, diminished, or disregarded in the shuffle. The focus shifts instead to the upset hispanic. Upset White people? No big deal. In fact, nobody even wonders whether White people as a people might be upset. They'll deal with it as they always do: look the other way, hide their heads in the sand, or blame themselves. If there are 12 to 20 million illegal immigrants (invaders) in the United States, it is our fault, so the mental sickness goes, since we built such a prosperous country that would naturally attract millions of people to come here illegally like bugs to a bug zapper. In other words, the responsibility lies with *us* somehow that these millions are here rather than with the millions who knowingly came here in violation of our laws in the first place. It is always our fault.

If "families have been divided," that too is somehow our fault because when the invaders crossed our borders illegally in the first place, we didn't ask them to bring the rest of their family members! We neglected to tell them to hitch a wagon and place grandma and their cousins in it so it's our fault that they stayed behind in Mexico. This is the insane thinking of our times. So, if some of the illegal immigrant invaders seek to become citizens, we are expected to allow a process by which the relatives they left behind in Mexico can become citizens too. If we don't, we allegedly "lack compassion" and are "breaking up families" that the invaders themselves of course broke up in the first place by coming here. *We are hence supposed to show more regard for their families than they themselves did.* The minds of our people are in chains.

If an illegal immigrant invader dies of thirst while crossing the desert border into America, that too is allegedly our fault since we failed to provide drinking water along the route. If an illegal invader dies of appendicitis because he was afraid to "come out of the shadows" due to his illegal presence in the country, it is allegedly our fault that he didn't feel comfortable enough (due to our allegedly wicked system) to come out of those shadows and seek that needed health care. If an illegal immigrant invader drowns while attempting to swim the Rio Grande, it is our fault that we didn't have a lifeguard on duty.

We are expected to know how to speak mestizo Spanish if we deal with illegal immigrants in any capacity, whether as border agents, policemen, or health care workers. If we don't, well, that's our fault too. We must always conform to them, not them to us. We must always cater to their (non-existent) "rights," never them to *our* rights. At this rate, it will eventually reach the point where if an illegal immigrant invader suffers a needle from a cactus while pawing his way across the border, we will be expected to come running with the tweezers.

If the minds of our White people were not in chains, none of this would be possible. White people would openly admit that they don't want more (mestizo) hispanics to come here as much as the (mestizo) hispanics openly admit that they do. There would be no talk whatever of "amnesty" because amnesty basically means that people are forgiven for breaking the law. There would be no reluctance to deport any and all known illegal immigrant invaders and far fewer claims that doing so would be "impractical"; if it was practical enough for them to invade the country in the first place, it is surely just as practical to deport them; if they could gradually trickle in by the millions, they can be gradually trickled *out* by the millions as well. White people would feel no obligation to learn the language of their invaders. White people would not be hesitant to ask suspected illegal immigrants for their papers proving that they are in fact here legally. White people would not feel obligated to provide education and health care to them, nor an obligation to quench their thirst nor feed their bellies. A people that is truly free is not only free to make its own laws but also feels itself free to discriminate with its compassion. Forced compassion is not compassion at all but rather, slavery.

A free people does not have to justify its laws to any other people. It does not ask any other people, "Is this law okay with you?" The law, rather, exists for *them*, not the outsider and not the racial minority in what is allegedly a democracy where the will of the majority is supposed to be paramount. A free people does not cower under the criticisms of other peoples but rather forges its own laws and its own destiny regardless of whatever criticisms by other peoples may be in the offing. It owes nobody but itself. And yet we witness in America the bizarre spectacle in which the Mexican government routinely protests to the American government its "displeasure" concerning American immigration policy, with the American government granting a hearing on the subject to which the Mexican government is not even remotely entitled. Such is the abnormal normalcy of our times that we allow an invasion of our country and periodically wine and dine the government of the country from whence the invaders came while that government campaigns for a response to the invasion that is more to its liking.

With the minds of our White people in chains though, some of our people even seem to think that doing "good" by the other races *justifies* that they do *bad to* their own interests as a people and yes, race. Thus these individuals, for example, scramble to do "right" by the illegal brown invaders knowing *full well* that they are doing *wrong* by their own people. Indeed, not only are they willing to do so but they are positively avid about it. They positively gloat as they spread the word that White people will soon be a minority within what was once their own land, that the Mexican invaders "take the jobs that Americans (White people) don't want," that they themselves have integrated their neighborhoods

26

and schools, that they themselves have adopted non-white children, and even that, to their greatest delight, they themselves have mixed their own bloodline with that of non-whites. They seem to have a suicidal death wish, a self-inflicted genocide in their hearts and minds. Nobody ever said, for example, that the racial integration of the public schools would be good for White people; such a thought never even entered the White so-called "civil rights workers" minds. Instead, their professed altruism *excluded their own people. Nobody* in fact believed or even argued that White students would receive an improved education by virtue of sitting alongside black students. Rather, what allegedly would benefit *black* students was the sole focus and concern. These individuals exist by the thousands, maybe even the millions. They are willing and happy to "reduce the achievement gap" between White and black students, for example, *even if it means pulling the achievement of Whites down in order to do it.* Such is the mania of "equality" that they would sacrifice *quality* in order to achieve it, including the future of their own people.

Similarly, no one thought that the racial integration of formerly exclusively White neighborhoods would result in less crime and less social strife. Rather, it was in fact tacitly acknowledged that the result would be more crime and more social strife (for White people) but that since the black newcomers would benefit from rubbing elbows with White people (allegedly), the integration of the neighborhoods was "socially desirable," with what is "socially desirable" being determined exclusively with reference to the best interests of blacks alone. So, every zoning law and every personal property right that had kept neighborhoods exclusively White were struck down in deference to everybody (non-whites) but the very White people who lived in those neighborhoods. New supposed "constitutional rights" were conjured up by those simply hell-bent upon foisting their own psychotic agenda upon a people they had come to hate: *their own.* To this day, the propagandized masses think that the Constitution somehow requires the integration of the races in schools and communities when in reality no such integration constitutional right exists, for if it did, we never would have needed a court to say that it did!

Similarly, no one thinks that today's fad of adoption of non-white children by White couples (especially so-called "celebrities") is somehow of benefit to White people; the idea never even enters the adopters' heads, in fact. Instead there is the almost maniacal drive to give love to a non-white child, to provide a home for a non-white child. The adopters, on the other hand, never even reflect that their adoption of the non-white child means the *non*-adoption of a *White* child. In other words, a White child did *not* receive their love or a home because of their preference for the non-White child. They fail to realize the truism that discrimination in *favor* of one entity (the non-white child) automatically results in discrimination *against* another entity (the White child). In economics, this principle is undeniable and is called the "opportunity cost" and yet in regards to our White people itself, it is always forgotten. It amounts to this: if you choose one opportunity, you are *always* forsaking another. If you choose to benefit another race you are *always* forsaking benefit to your own race in the particular situation at hand. One of the most basic principles of economics is sadly passed blindly by when it comes to the well-being of our people itself; people indeed fail to realize that there is a "cost" to our own people when we help others, that is, when they are cognizant of their own people's existence at all! The bottom line is that these non-white adopters would rather have a child of a different race than that of their own race. Their inclinations have turned from the natural (preference for their own kind) to the unnatural (preference for a different kind). In no other race is this seen: blacks do not go out of their way to adopt White children, for example; indeed such a thing is practically unheard of. This is because, unlike Whites, the minds of blacks are not in chains; they do not feel any calling to benefit non-blacks, do not feel guilty for supposed sins against non-blacks in need of penitence, do not mock and ridicule the color of their own skin, and would prefer instead to see the black race benefitted in all things and at all times. Would that our White people rediscover and embrace such a simple, basic, and natural psyche! Blacks in fact tend to think it odd that White people feel compelled to adopt black children; they cannot understand or relate to such a bizarre (and idiotic) altruism and sometimes wonder if there is instead some kind of ulterior motive at work whether conscious or unconscious. "Why do these White people want to raise our children?" they ask themselves. "Do they wish to strip them of their black cultural identity?" "Do they wish to parade their tokens around to show what supposedly holier than thou do-gooders they are?" "Do they wish to dispel any notion that they are racist?" Thus blacks themselves wonder at this strange "cross-racial" adoption business. The other races do the same. Some even wonder whether it is some kind of conspiracy to deracinate the most vulnerable of their own racial community but no, the answer simply lies in White mental befuddlement.

This befuddlement reaches its most severe form in those White people who partake in the ultimate form of betrayal of their own kind by breeding outside of their race, often with the very conscious desire to strike a blow against it. The individual who commits suicide does so often times with the belief that he lacks sufficient value as a person to justify his continuing to exist. No less is this true of those who commit *racial* suicide through interracial marriage; he or she does not believe that his or her race possesses sufficient value to justify its continued existence and thus partakes in an act that destroys it. There is thus just as much hatred and lack of esteem bound up with the one as with the other even if this is not even remotely hinted at or realized in today's so-called mainstream society. Prior generations knew this of course. They knew that interracial sexual relations were a form of rebellion, of perversion grounded in the hatred possessed by this transgressor of the racial community, and they consequently made it a criminal offense. Thus, contrary to the overwhelming yet deluded belief today that the hatred rested with those who made such laws, the hatred actually rested with those willing and even eager to destroy their White bloodline through the breeding of mixed-race children. It was they who sought to destroy, after all, while the lawmakers sought to preserve, and should we not, as a matter of basic logic, favor that which preserves our people rather than that which destroys it? The individual who would deny this is the individual whose mind is also in chains; by the same token, we may as well dismantle the military, police forces, hospitals, and other entities which also seek to preserve our people. We might as well call all of these institutions "hateful." It simply cannot be denied that the progeny of an interracial sexual union cannot be White and thus rather than replicating her own kind as her ancestors did before her, the White woman who has committed this deed has suddenly and absolutely forsaken her ancestry and made herself a renegade to her own people. Such a deed would simply not be possible without a feeling of hate and lack of esteem for the people to whom she belongs. Even if it is true that the White woman (or man) loves the non-white spouse, what people neglect to realize is that this love is only a consequence of a prior hatred, lack of esteem for, and disregard for her (his) own people! In other words, interracial marriage does not occur because the individual of one race just happens to "fall in love" with an individual of another race. Rather, there is first a hatred, lack of esteem, and disregard for one's own race that makes such a love possible. Thus White women who breed outside their race will frequently candidly voice their contempt and derision for White men as part of the explanation for their actions and White men who breed outside their race will do the same concerning White women. Have we not heard from White women, for example, that White men are less virile and masculine than black men and from White men that yellow ("Asian") women make more obedient wives than supposedly assertive White women? The disdain for their own people is clear. When the normal loses its luster, then does the abnormal sparkle.

Of course, the fact that White people are so humiliated in the present society has gone a long way towards removing that very luster of breeding within one's own kind. The White man is no longer considered the elite of the world but rather "just a White guy" as if there is something inherently lacking in him, as if his being is of very little consequence. Businesses are run by "old white males" as if they are somehow defective on that basis. White people are supposedly "privileged," are supposedly lucky to have everything they have, and have merely benefitted by fortuitous circumstances in getting ahead of the supposedly more deserving toiling black or hispanic. This is the undercurrent throughout the entire society. White men are supposedly weak pencil-pushers sitting at their desks all day while the virile Negro "actually does all the work." Their skin is "pasty" while that of the Negro is supposedly the epitome of health. The White woman is supposedly the bossy nagger uninterested in femininity while the Oriental woman is supposedly docile, subservient, and ready for every beck and call, the hispanic woman is supposedly a "hot Latin" imbued with some kind of mystical sexual expertise, and the Negro woman supposedly "knows how to treat her man." It is little wonder that with all of these overt and not so overt negative messages about their own people bombarding them that so many of our White brethren have betrayed their White race through interracial breeding accordingly.

Some years ago a film came out entitled "White Men Can't Jump." Aside from the author and a few others "on the fringe," nobody had nary a word to say about the obviously racist nature of the film's title. What though do you think the reaction would have been if a film had come out instead with the title of "Black Men Can't Think"? The outcry would have been deafening and White people would have played a major role in that outcry. A theater would have been lucky to have successfully aired such an entitled film without protests, violence, or worse. In other words, the state of affairs is such that while a black film director can comfortably issue a film that mocks the athletic ability of White men and do so without any controversy, a White film director cannot comfortably issue a film that mocks the intellectual ability of black men. Worse still, he can expect the wrath of *White* people if he were to dare make such a film, wrath nowhere to be found when *White* people are the ones being mocked. What is good for the goose is simply not good for the gander in this misbegotten society. The minds of our White people are indeed in chains. They will raise their voices to defend others but not themselves. They will clench a fist to defend others but not themselves. They will even give their lives for the rights of others but not for the rights of themselves.

If black and brown racism is acceptable, then White racism should be acceptable too. By all means, let us admit that blacks have a natural superiority in certain sports—which is obvious to all who have eyesight—but let us also admit that Whites have a natural superiority in intellect which, though less visually obvious, is just as substantiated by the evidence. White men may well not be able to jump as high as black men on the basketball court but by the same token, black men may not be able to think as deeply as White men. Either both propositions are "racist" or neither of them are racist; one cannot be racist but the other not and yet the society of today would have it that racism is exclusively a province of White people, an idea that is quite quaint for the black and brown racists of course but absolutely disempowering for the White people of whom we are a part. White people are "allowed" to comment on the superior ability of blacks in certain sports but disallowed from commenting on their own intellectual superiority. If this is not a plain, simple example of the double-standard in this society, it is difficult to conceive of what would be.

What though does "racism" even mean? Other than a biased and false dictionary definition, it is a word that is bandied about without anyone bothering to explore its actual meaning and, as a result, it is one of the most ill-construed words that there is. All "racism" in reality means is the practice of racial distinctions and thus the "racist" is one who makes racial distinctions, whether positive or negative. Thus the National Association for the Advancement of Colored People is plainly a racist organization because it distinguishes between "colored" people and White people. In other words, it is concerned with race and thus is *ipso facto* "racist." The use of "racism" and especially "racist" as pejoratives is quite simply misplaced. Whether the NAACP likes White people too, thinks that White people are equal or whatever is irrelevant; since it is concerned with race, it is racist, and so is every other of the thousands of non-white organizations that exist. Racism itself has nothing to do with hatred, race superiority, or any other perceived negative sentiment. The black NAACP is racist, the brown National Council of La Raza ("The Race") is racist, the White Ku Klux Klan is racist, "affirmative action" policies are racist, and even the U.S. census is racist (as it too makes racial distinctions) since all of these groups and policies make distinctions on the grounds of race. There is nothing negative about racism, inherently.

The same applies to "discrimination." There is nothing inherently negative about the word, a word that simply means the making of choices. Whenever you go to a grocery store, you discriminate as to which products to buy. When you marry, you discriminate as to whom you believe is desirable as a mate for life. When you drive to work, you discriminate as to the route you think is the best to get there. When you watch television, you discriminate in your choice of channels. When you read a book, you are discriminating in your choice of titles. All life involves discrimination, the making of choices. One can often fault the choice made itself, to be sure, but one cannot fault the choosing. To ban all "discrimination" in society would ban all choosing and thus render men total slaves, for is it not true that the slave in chains has likewise been deprived of all choice in how to live? Thus people should think twice before trumpeting "a world without discrimination" and other such twaddle when the reality is that a life as free men *absolutely requires it.* No free man can so much as pass a single day of his life without discriminating.

All discrimination (i.e. the making of choices) likewise involves the choosing of one thing at the *expense* of another. Recall the "opportunity cost" discussed earlier. When you choose regular gasoline at the gas station, you are *not* choosing premium gasoline. When you choose to dine at *this* restaurant, you are *not* choosing to dine at *that* restaurant. When you are choosing to read *my* book, you are *not* choosing to read *someone else's* book. Thus all choices are acts of "discrimination" and all discrimination encompasses acts of choosing. One choice is implemented and the others are not. No one would actually want a life without the ability to make choices, i.e. to discriminate. To wake up in the morning and not be able to choose what to eat, not to be able to choose what to read, where to work, where to live, and a thousand other choices per day; such a life free from "discrimination" would not be worth living. It would be the slave's life. *It is in the very nature of slavery that the slave is not allowed to make choices. It is in the very nature of freedom that the free man is.*

So, let us dispense with the almost mystically negative connotation of the words "racism" and "discrimination" which are, in fact, used to keep the minds of our White people in chains. Is it not a fact for example that the minute a White man tries to assert anything even remotely favorable to White people that accusations of "racism" are heard? And yet the blacks and browns can, and do, do the same thing (assert matters favorable to their respective races) all the time with no cries of "racism" forthcoming. The same of course happens with "discrimination": White people are discriminated against in business and schools and by the government across America but this has Orwellistically been renamed "affirmative action," while, on the other hand, the minute one White man somewhere has the temerity to actually say that he doesn't want to sell his home to blacks, cries of "discrimination" screech from the airwaves and one would think that the fellow had just committed a capital offense. Is the double-standard not obvious? And how long will we remain enchained to it? How long will we continue to tolerate the massive discrimination *against* our own people everywhere while at the same time refusing to discriminate *for* it? Why must we be the only race that practices forbearance when it comes to our own best interests?

In reality, every act of discrimination *in favor* of a particular group is discrimination *against* another so let's quit being weak in this regard! If the blacks and browns wish to discriminate (choose) in favor of their own kind, more power to them but don't whine when White people want to discriminate in favor of their own kind too. And White people, do not deny to your own people what you would freely give to the others! Such is sickness, such is mind perversion. Everything about our society points in the direction that our White people are on their way out and yet instead of protesting and resisting such a dispossession and demise, many of our own people are applauding it. With friends like these, who needs foes? The lack of a pure and proud White people is alleged to be a blessing to aspire to, a blessing somehow consonant with American values, and indeed is somehow the natural evolution of American society as if even a single one of our Founding Fathers would not be disappointed at the turn that their country has taken were they to have the misfortune to be able to witness it. Did they really fight for United States of America where their descendants would be expected to forego any and all choices in their own favor as a race while the other races do anything but in *their* favor? Did they really seek to create a country where their descendants would one day grovel before the other races' every whim? Did they really want us to become second class citizens in our own land? Now we do not even feel free to discriminate as to who enters our (former) country and thus takes possession of it! Is that the kind of "freedom" that our Founding Fathers had in mind?

You must understand that "racism" and "discrimination" have been used simply as smear words to discourage White people from doing for themselves what the other races do without objection. There is nothing negative about the words inherently but through repetitive propaganda, White people have been deceived and indeed coerced into avoiding, at all cost, any kind of living that could even *possibly* invoke these supposedly bad words from being hurled at them since the words are (erroneously) thought to denote reprehensible conduct. The words have become an evil in themselves to avoid without justification, with White people being distracted by the words instead of being conscious of the true issues behind them. Lost has been the fact that non-whites practice racism and discrimination, for example, and that there exists no reasoned basis for White people not to do the same. "Equality" is simply no legitimate object; the fact that non-whites practice racism and discrimination as a means to (allegedly) raise themselves does not mean that White people should not practice racism and discrimination as a means to raise *themselves* as well, or that they should not *refuse* to practice racism and discrimination in favor of the non-whites in an effort to lower themselves so as to attain "equality." In reality, our refusal to practice racism and discrimination for our own people has only lowered our own self-esteem and self-worth as a people, for it entails the abandonment of all feeling on its behalf.

When it comes to much trumpeted "diversity," the true idea behind it is that there are *too many White people* and that this state of affairs, in itself, reveals that the society in question is somehow inferior to the so-called "multi-cultural" society. In other words, once again White people are set upon, derided, and condemned because of their very Whiteness, that of their neighbors, and that of their communities. The sick mentality of our times says that it is not enough that White people support the other races with their taxes, not enough that we feel guilty for all of our supposed sins against them, not enough that we open wide our borders to them, and on and on, but that we must also break up every White community, everywhere, with so-called "diversity." Our ancestors lived in all-White communities throughout their past thousands of years of history without ever having the feeling that they were being deprived of something and yet now we are somehow supposed to feel empty at the thought that our communities may "only" be composed of members of our own kind! It is said that we "lack diversity" as if this were some kind of ailment. "Oh my goodness, there are only White people here! We need to 'fix' this situation by 'bringing people of color' to our community. Without experiencing 'diversity,' our children will be disadvantaged. Let's bring in some nice Somalis, Vietnamese, Guatemalans, or somebody else to fix things because my children will miss out if 'all' they see are White people!" Such is the sickness, the self-hatred, the well-nigh idiocy of our times. Our people are simply not considered whole or complete without the presence of the others. Without the other races living around us and in our midst, life would even be "boring," so it is said. *The message is thus sent that we are inferior.* After all, if we cannot be whole people and live whole lives without the presence of non-whites amongst us, what does that say about us? Inferiority! Across America, communities are targeted for their Whiteness and are in fact ridiculed for it. The clear presumption is that White communities are missing something, that they are defective, that they lack the supposed "enrichment" of the multi-racial community. Whenever the results of the census are reported, there are comments about how this or that state or community "still" lacks diversity and what can be done to change that, the word "diversity" confined exclusively to the *White* areas of the country. The State of Vermont, for example, is said to be "*still* one of the least diverse states" with the clear implication that this is some kind of problem, that it is "lagging behind," and that it had better hurry up and become more "diverse." States such as Montana and the Dakotas are regularly made fun of because of their Whiteness. Notably as well, states with a heavy White population are never deemed politically important and thus are routinely ignored in presidential elections. In sum, White communities and states are chastised, ridiculed, and devalued for a supposed lack of "diversity." Our Whiteness, as always, is a defect, a blemish, a misfortune in need of repair. The minds of our people are in chains.

Never though is this said to the non-whites. Nobody ever says to a black community that it is deficient because it is lacking White people, and that it needs to "celebrate diversity" by bringing them in. Nobody ever says to the hispanic community, "you need to 'enrich' your community by 'diversifying' it with Whites and blacks." Nobody ever feels a pressing need to integrate black, brown, and yellow communities with White people, only the other way around. Nobody says to China that its population is too yellow. No one says to Saudi Arabia that it is too Arab. No one says to Africa that it is too black. On the contrary, the Whites who live in Africa are often told that they need to pack their bags and leave, if that courtesy is extended to them at all, in order to make way for black people. Thus "diversity" is only a *White* problem and it is only a *White* problem because only *White* people have their minds in chains. *It is not the lack of diversity in our communities and states that is the flaw but rather the thought that we need it.* Yes we have an ailment but it is an ailment of the *mind*, not an excess of White people in our communities and states! Why else would White people be the only people that practically cries with anguish when it encounters "a lack of diversity," and only within its own communities and states at that, while the other races do not? It is because of the sickness of our minds. We are a people that has come to despise itself and thus considers itself sorely in need of the others who feel no such need. Nearly everyone in the country of China is of the yellow race—more than 99.99 percent—and everybody is fine with that but the minute a mere all-White *community* is discovered in the United States and elsewhere, *White* people abound lamenting its lack of "diversity." Yes, the minds of our people are in chains.

In the realm of professional sports, commentators lament the dearth of blacks in hockey but no one laments and criticizes the dearth of White people on a basketball court. Those who wish to push blacks into hockey are nowhere to be found when it comes to complaining about the almost complete absence of White people in an NBA game. In other words, once again, White people are told that they need diversity but no such demand is made of another race. I have heard sports commentators express their wish that there were more black hockey players but never have I heard a sports commentator express his wish that there were more Whites on an NBA basketball court. The sports commentator who did would probably be fired from his job for being "insensitive" and so many a tongue is held in check even if his brain *is* capable of formulating the thought. The message that is sent is a clear one: White people are of less value than non-whites, that it's unfortunate that there aren't more blacks in hockey but quite fine that blacks are the only players on the basketball court. In other words, we want more blacks so as to be more "diverse" when an overwhelming White sport is at issue but we couldn't care less about diversity when an overwhelming black sport is at issue.

Thus *only Whites* must diversify, i.e. make way for non-whites, while non-whites can remain mono-racial at will. We have become so accustomed to the situation, to the double-standard, that few of us even notice it. In essence, we White people are incessantly told in one form or fashion or another that we should make way for the other races but never, quite simply never, are the other races told that they should make way for us. There is nothing that we are allowed to call our own but plenty they are allowed to call *their* own. This is an odd sort of "equality," is it not? And yet this is the mental slavery that has come over us.

Even in terms of nomenclature the other races are favored over us. Some years ago, for example, black leaders decided that one word was not enough to describe their people, that they should henceforward be referred to as "African-American." No such change was instituted for White people of course. "African-American" was alleged to be more respectful but in this 'respectful' mood, the thought that maybe White people should likewise be afforded an analogous token of respect never entered anybody's head or if it did, nobody had the temerity to say so. Let the reader ask himself, when was the last time you heard of a White person being referred to as a "European-American?" Whether "European-American" really is more respectful than "White" is not the point; rather, the point is that society has come to view "African-American" as more respectful than "black" without any analogous consideration for the respect of White people at all. Indeed, a White man is a thousand times more likely to be referred to as "just a White guy" than as a "European-American" and yet how many people though would refer to a black man as "just a black guy"? White people who would feel perfectly comfortable in referring to the males of their own kind as "just" White guys in public company would manifestly *not* feel comfortable referring to the males of the black race as "just" black guys in the same public company, or even in most private company for that matter. No, consideration of respect is decidedly one-sided: away from ourselves. White people are devalued. It is almost a mindset that there are *too many* of us, even though we are actually a tiny minority in this world. There are Whites who are extremely careful to always refer to blacks as "African-Americans" and who visibly appear to be uncomfortable with themselves when they now and then forget. No such care and consideration is to be found though when they refer to their own people. Indeed, some of the same White people who so conscientiously utter the term "African-American" in one sentence have no hesitation in uttering the words "white trash" in the next. They are so unwilling to in any way besmirch the sentiments of another race and yet they *are* willing to besmirch their own race! The implication in all of this is quite simply that White people are worthy of less respect than black people and no one bothers to challenge such a notion. In the name of combating alleged hate and prejudice, so much of it has been turned upon ourselves.

The White man who *loves* his White Race and its culture, on the other hand, receives a double-dose of the hatred of the current society, ironically enough, for not only is contempt leveled at him simply by virtue of his mere membership in the devalued, derided, and guilt-ridden White Race but his refusal to hate his own kind essentially doubles his intrinsic "error" of Whiteness in itself. In other words, it is bad enough that he is White at all but to be *proud* to be White is, in the minds of a White people currently in chains, like a criminal who remains proud of his crimes. Then some kind of remorse is expected and when it is not forthcoming, the "crime" of White self-value is hated all the more, as well as its "perpetrators" of course. Thus we face the dual irony that not only are White people afflicted with a self-hatred, or at least self-contempt, today, but that those White people who instead love themselves as a people are targeted with hatred for precisely that love. Racial hatred is blessed in the current society so long as White people *direct it at themselves* but if they are perceived or claimed to direct it at another race, or indeed merely love their own race, they are hated additionally for it. Some of the most hateful people you will ever witness are thus, oddly enough, the very people who claim to be the most against hate. You yourself may be one of them but because you so adamantly campaign against what you perceive as hate, you do not reflect upon how much you yourself hate in the process.

The logic is certainly an odd one: "I hate you for loving White people," but even if the logic were actually "I hate you for hating the other races," as is often (erroneously) claimed, this too makes little sense for if hatred is bad, hating people for hating must also be bad. In fact, hating White people for allegedly hating other races makes even *less* sense than hating someone for loving his own race because what is deemed so objectionable in the first place (the emotion of hatred) is repeated in the objector who then logically should hate himself for hating! The wheel of mental confusion thus goes round and round. The flaw in the thinking rests with hating someone for hating in the first place and yet all the while the alleged hatred thought to be so objectionable isn't really hatred at all but rather, self-love. In sum, harboring a negative emotion towards someone for that someone himself allegedly harboring a negative emotion is problematic, to say the least, and it becomes downright sad when it turns out that the person was misjudged in the first place! The prime motivation of every White man who loves his White Race and its culture is none other than the preservation of same. Should he really be a target of hatred for feeling this love? If he were really a hater, he would not attach himself to his race and culture, for attachment is a form of *love*, not hatred. The current society has totally missed this fundamental point and slashes its own hate-driven swords at a phantom largely of its own making.

As for the vaunted so-called "institutions of higher learning," the minds of our young people are conditioned by propaganda to despise having to learn about "dead white males" in conjunction with a push to remove these "dead white males" from the curriculum. Again, the message is that White people, and especially White males, have been overvalued and that they must now, accordingly, be *de*valued. The less obvious implication is that White men should exit the stage of life, now! Colleges abound with racial pride (in the form of myriad non-white organizations) but none of it is White. Again, if this is "equality," it is a very strange sort. There are "Black Student Unions," for example, on college campuses across the United States but it is doubtful that there is even a single "White Student Union." Since all expression of White racial pride and advocacy is mentally and socially suppressed in our society, few if anybody even tries to form such an organization and if they did try, it would likely be barred outright by the college administration or, even more likely, the students would fail to find a member of the faculty willing to serve as faculty advisor as colleges almost universally require for campus groups. How many White college professors are willing to attach their names to groups likely to be smeared as "racist," after all? Thus there is a lock on the brain and lock on the door while the other races can go in and out of their doors of racial advocacy at will.

The word "nigger," for its part, is today considered as the worst word that anybody can utter, worse even than the F-word and other profanity with a sexual connotation. Practically universally, people are under the impression that it is a smear word, used at all times, at least by White people, to demean an oppressed and otherwise victimized black race. We have all been led to believe that the word has some kind of inherent power to psychologically maim those at whom it is directed, that it is, in essence, a word used only with deliberation by evil people, perhaps the type of people who would drown kittens or who would gnash their teeth late at night at the thought that there are people happy in the world. Thus, in sum, usage of the word today is almost considered some kind of poison, reserved for the diabolical or perhaps the ignorant or feeble-minded, that no one uses the word without being disturbed in some way or keen upon disturbing others. This of course is the propaganda with which we have all been fed from the media, the schools, and the government. Society naturally and necessarily follows. Tellingly, the most scourged word in America is one that supposedly maligns *black* people, not a word that maligns White people or any other race for that matter. This is highly symptomatic of our mental slavery, that the minds of our people are in chains. And consider the fact that White people seem to get more worked up by the usage of the word than the blacks themselves! Thus the word calls for discussion within these pages, perhaps the only place it can receive such treatment free from societal taboos.

In reality, there are probably few words that have been as wrongly maligned as this one. The idea that it was originally used to speak ill of a black person is untrue and it has, in fact, only been deemed a "racial slur" in recent history. In essence, no black man was offended by being referred to as a "nigger" until somebody told him that he should be. Nor was the word ever confined to the South or confined to the institution of slavery. It was used in the United States, it was used in Europe, and it was used all over the world. Nor is the word a derivation of the word "Negro" as so many people have been led to believe. Nor is the word "nigger" a corruption of the word "Negro" either as is also commonly claimed. Not only is practically everything that people think of when they consider the word "nigger" false but they also have passed blindly by the reality of the word even though it is nearly in front of their face.

Here then is the reality: it is not that the word derives from the word "Negro" but rather the opposite: the word "Negro" derives from the word "niger," the Latin word for "*black*"! Thousands of years before any African slaves were being brought to America, the classical Roman people used the Latin word "niger" which was, and is, pronounced exactly the same as the word "nigger" which is merely a slightly different spelling of the same word in the English speaking world. Nigger, like niger, thus simply means "black." There is no more inherent contempt or animosity in the word than in any other denoting a color. There are in fact two nation-states in Africa today whose names derive from "niger": Niger and Nigeria. Their names are no more racial slurs than "nigger" is; that they are pronounced by the inhabitants and others differently than the original Latin word is pronounced (nig-er) is of no consequence. That the Latin word for black is "niger," pronounced exactly the same as "nigger," is simply too much to be a coincidence concerning the origin of the latter word. Niger (black) equals nigger (black).

It is thus remarkable that a mere brief study of the Latin language, upon which so many languages of Europe are based or influenced, overturns the entire (false) reputation of this so-castigated word. Furthermore, the Latin language was widely used throughout Europe in matters of scholarship and diplomacy up until the 18th century, long after classical Rome was no more. Hence the word niger/nigger is simply a holdover from that language. When White people reached sub-Saharan Africa during the Age of Exploration, they used Latin words to describe the places and people they encountered including "niger," naturally enough, to describe the inhabitants and the word simply carried over to the Western hemisphere later. White Englishmen, specifically, would use both the words '"black" and "nigger" (with the extra "g") interchangeably to refer to them, as well as the Spanish "negro" for that matter, the latter two words simply meaning "black" in the Latin and Spanish languages respectively. It is possible that "nigger" became a preferred word in reference to a black person (even George Washington used it) because it is more of a noun than an adjective; in other words, while it is unclear what somebody might mean by saying "the black crossed the street" (the black what?), it is not unclear what somebody means by saying "the nigger crossed the street" as "nigger" (niger), formerly an adjective simply denoting a color, gradually became a noun denoting a member of a particular race. In other words, since one word could be used to describe that person, it had a natural advantage over other, longer terms as word choice tends to be guided more by utility than by anything else. Thus, putting aside all emotions—emotions that were indeed not a factor at all at the time since the word had no negative connotation—it was easier to say "nigger" in reference to someone than "black man," quite simply. By the same token, it is easier to say "fired" than "discharged from employment," "foreigner" than "citizen from another country," and many other terms that we have very matter of factly come to employ for the sake of ease of language. No slur was intended nor given.

Today though in the days of our mentally enslaved White

people, White people are afraid to even engage in a discussion of the word, are afraid to utter it, and sometimes even try to pull books from school libraries that mention it like *The Adventures of Huckleberry Finn* and others, the former even though the context clearly shows that Tom was not insulting his friend "Nigger Jim" when he referred to him that way any more than he would have done so had he used the words "Black Jim" instead, "Nigger Jim" and "Black Jim" meaning exactly the same thing. (Indeed, the author Mark Twain was very sympathetic to and supportive of blacks in America throughout his writings and throughout his life and would not have used the word "nigger" if the word were really a racial slur as it has so wrongly been made out to be.) Blacks ("niggers") must further be amused at how fearful White people have become over a word that is used often in their own community, a fact that also demonstrates that it cannot truly be the word of insult that it has been claimed and assumed to be, foisted upon the world by White people out to demean. Notably also, blacks only seem to take great offense at the word when *White* people use it rather than when their own people use it and this too would seem to indicate that the problem is not the word itself. Strangely enough, historical figures of renown like Abraham Lincoln are criticized for having used the word, as well as looked at askance for it, without anyone stopping to think that maybe, just maybe, the word wasn't viewed as insultive in the first place and hence why he and so many others used the word so freely and routinely and without a second thought at that. It would be interesting to discover whether any black historical figures used the word as well and whether they too are criticized for it or not. Probably no criticism would be forthcoming. The idea though that blacks past and present have only called themselves niggers with some frequency because they (still) bear the alleged torment, the scar of White oppression, should be treated as the nonsense that it is; what is more sad though is that there are White people who believe such tripe! And it so happens that some of the most intelligent of our race have their brains the most in chains. They bow, they scrape, and they appease as a consequence even with regard to mere suppositions that are foolish on their face. Some of the same people are willing to say "white trash" but begin to turn green at the thought of saying the word "nigger." They will tiptoe around any possibility that they may offend blacks and yet are willing to leap in offense to their own people. The poor black in their eyes is "oppressed" while the poor White is "white trash". This is the sickness of our times.

A race that is unwilling to use words of its own choice for fear of offending other races is not free. Even if the word "nigger" were not the neutral word that it actually is, our White people would be right to use it at their leisure just as much as any other word, and just as much as any other race uses the word for that matter. Far more important than the word is the principle. Only when our people feel free to say the word "nigger" once again can it be said that they are free. We are, after all, talking about a mere word. Our fear of it is highly symbolic of our weakness and our slavery. There is, after all, no other word that we are afraid to say and fear is a form of bondage, is it not? Even in criticizing the word, our people won't say it today; instead, they will refer to "the n-word" as if saying "nigger" were some kind of verbal leprosy. If the situation weren't so illustrative of the mental slavery of our White people today, it would be laughable. With great seriousness and earnestness, they avoid saying the word "nigger" as a vampire would avoid a cross. It is just a word, for goodness sakes, and are we a race of men or are we a race of rabbits? The word simply denotes a color and the (black) race that bears it.

Though we as White people today certainly do not feel privileged to use certain words that those filled with misplaced righteousness have declared "verboten," how often have we heard the word "privileged" as a sort of code word for White people, with it sometimes even being said that simply by being White, we are "privileged" in life? Tell that to the White man who is working two or more jobs just to keep his family fed, housed, and clothed. Tell that to the White single mother who struggles to find a babysitter who doesn't charge nearly as much as her own wages.

Tell that to the White men whose job is that of digging coal from the bowels of the earth whose wage is a pitiful fraction of that of black actors, black sports players, and black talk show hosts. Tell that to the White construction worker who, like the White coal miner, routinely risks his very life on the job. "Privileged"? The word when used in regard to our White people implies that we didn't work for what we have, that what we have came from the toil of others. Is not though the black man who makes (not earns) tens of millions of dollars per year by bouncing a ball on a floor and tossing it into a basket, privileged? Is not a certain black talk show host whose "net worth" is over a *billion* dollars privileged? Are not the thousands and perhaps millions of blacks who have their employment and position of employment due to government discrimination in their favor, privileged? Are not the millions of illegal Mexican invaders who could have been met at the border with gunfire by the U.S. Army privileged to instead be given a job, free education, and free health care? Are not the millions of Orientals who fled communist Vietnam, China, and elsewhere and given asylum and citizenship here also privileged? Are not the millions of non-whites from abroad who are allowed to attend our colleges privileged? And how many people realize that there are more poor White people in America than any other race?

We as White people never had to favor blacks in employment. We never had to allow "illegal immigrants" jobs, free education, and free health care. We never had to allow any Orientals into the U.S.; in fact, we never had to allow *any* non-white immigration of any kind. We never had to allow non-whites from abroad "student visas" so that they could come here and be educated in our schools. In other words, we gave all of these groups "privileges." Instead of a feeling of entitlement, there should rather be a feeling of *gratitude* on their part. And instead of us thinking that we as White people have not done enough for these groups, we should be thinking that we have done way, way too much.

It is not the White people who are privileged; rather, we

worked for what we have with few exceptions. Black slavery has been outlawed in America for over 140 years and those White people who actually profited by it—the very few—lost their wealth when it ended since their wealth was bound up with the very slaves who were freed. Furthermore, relatively few South-erners owned slaves in the first place. Besides, the South was nearly totally destroyed in the so-called "Civil War" and to this day it has not recovered its former economic status. Finding a White person who is wealthy ("privileged") today because his ancestors enslaved blacks would be like trying to find a needle in a haystack. This is the truth that society does not want talked about because those who manipulate the minds of the people would rather that we White people forever have our minds in chains of guilt, self-abnegation, and low self-esteem while maintaining in the non-white population the myth that we owe them something. "Atone" is the word that underlies every single policy involving the races with the Whites (wrongly) doing the atoning. In reality, we have nothing to atone for. If blacks are unhappy that their an-cestors were brought here as slaves, they should again consider the fact that it was *fellow Africans* who sold their ancestors into slavery and thus allot their blame in that direction accordingly. The idea that White people chased blacks into African jungles to enslave them—as portrayed in the fictional television series "Roots"—is indeed a myth. Rather, blacks were held in captivity by fellow blacks on the African shore, available for sale to all com-ers. Thus technically, White people did not even "enslave" blacks as they were already enslaved before Whites got there. We must thus ask why Whites should bear this strange burden for some-thing that very few Whites participated in and didn't cause in the first place while blacks hold themselves utterly (and conveniently) blameless in the matter. At the very least, responsibility is shared but when has that ever been acknowledged? A moment's pause for reflection would show that a few slave-traders could never have rounded up millions of Africans without the active and in-deed overwhelming collaboration of their fellow Africans. It makes little sense to blame the purchasers of enslaved persons more than those who took them by force into servitude in the first place, but of course blaming the White people of today for things that happened hundreds of years before they were born, including the notion that a collective debt has been incurred by us, makes less sense still. There was nothing especially unique about African slavery and nothing that justifies any sense of shame on the part of the White people living today. All races and cultures throughout history have practiced slavery and to this day, various African tribes *still* practice it. In other words, while it was *White* people who ended the enslavement of blacks in North America—after losing over 600,000 dead in a fratricidal war—*blacks have continued to practice it upon themselves in Africa.* Thus any White guilt over the matter is entirely misplaced. It may well be true that every person alive today, of whatever race, has an ancestor who was enslaved. So what? White people have gotten over it but blacks (and their numerous White liberal advocates) will not so long as they can use it to bludgeon White people with guilt to their own social, economic, and political advantage.

No matter what fault we may find with the institution or practice of *Negro* slavery, it is a fault that we should keep within our own household. In other words, *White people should never take the side of blacks against the memory of those White people in the past who owned black slaves.* All of the moral posturing of today does not give the present generation some kind of moral superiority or ascendancy over that of generations past. There should rather be some kind of loyalty towards our own kind. If White people in the past did things which we today find objectionable, they were still our people to whom we should have a sense of loyalty. A great American patriot once said, "My country, right or wrong." If this saying is reasonable and indeed laudable, let us consider why the saying "My Race, right or wrong" should be less so. Should we not, in fact, value our people itself even more than the soil on which they stand and the society in which they live? Discrimination is the law of life; it is difficult to conceive of anything more basic to life than the act of making choices, i.e. to discriminate. The only question is thus *how* we will discriminate, not whether we will or not. When it comes to our race, will we hence discriminate *for* it or will we discriminate *against* it? Which discrimination makes more sense? If we were black, brown, or yellow, it would be proper and wholeheartedly right to discriminate in favor of that which benefits the black, brown, and yellow races of the world and no one would even begin to object. By the same token then, why should we not discriminate in favor of that which benefits White people since we are indeed White? Should we not be comfortable enough with whom we are so as to be willing to advance *ourselves*?

Even in the realm of culture, we are today, sadly, discriminating against our own race. Is it not true that our White people of today have become so demoralized that our culture has become nigrified, in fact? White youth listen to black music, sometimes dress as blacks stereotypically do, and sometimes even ape the black in speech, things which blacks themselves understandably and laudably despise in White people. What could be more illustrative of so many befuddled White youth today than the young man wearing baggy clothes with pants falling down his waist, a ball cap on crooked, a Malcolm X t-shirt, speaking "ebonics," and listening to "rap" music? Is this a youth at home in White culture, comfortable with whom he really is as a White man, and proud of his White race? One hundred years ago that same youth, living in a far more healthy society that did not denigrate White people for being White, would have been listening to the music of Richard Wagner or some other composer of perhaps the greatest achievement that White people have accomplished in their history: classical music. Instead, in this present anarchical society, many of our youth have traded (though not consciously, to be sure) the pleasant strains of greatness for mindless cacophony that only destroys their soul and spirit. Their heroes are black, their idols are black, and their minds are likewise chained to the depths of the black abyss.

Nor is the sickness only confined to the so-called "wigger" youth: rather, *throughout* our society, the music that our people partake in is likewise nigrified. We in fact have the bizarre situation in which music sung by blacks sounds black and music sung by Whites sounds black too. "Pop" music is black and lest the fact be forgotten, "pop" stands for "popular." Hence the popular music of the day is *black* music performed by both black "artists" and White "artists." One can hear the song sung, assume that the singer is black, and then be confronted with the recording label showing that the singer is in fact White. And yet, to be blunt, what the hell is a White woman doing singing black gospel music, for example? Is it not a fact that these days you are far more likely to hear this than a White woman singing Ave Maria? Our whole psyche has become divested from our own culture. Even the Star Spangled Banner is not immune; the author considers himself lucky when he hears it sung by a White person who *doesn't* sing it as if it were a black gospel song! The way our White people are singing it these days, one would think that it must be a Negro spiritual or something rather than a song that was, in fact, written by *a White separatist* about White Americans defending against the White British in an 1814 naval bombardment. Underlying the White mimicry of black voices and black music is dissatisfaction with our own race and culture. It is not enough to sing a song anymore as our ancestors did; instead, we must "jazz it up" and throw a wild emotionalism into it that is actually foreign to our nature. In other words, we White people have come to view ourselves as plain, bland, uneventful, and unexciting in dire need of "soul," of "rhythm," of "spice" outside our own race. We supposedly have a deficit, a lack, a stuffiness when left to our own devices. The minds of our White people are indeed in chains. A formerly whole people is now a shell.

We have been told that White people lack a sense of rhythm. Tell that to the lovers of the music of Johann Sebastian Bach, Anton Bruckner, Peter Tchaikovsky, and numerous others who wrote rhythms far more intricate than anything that has ever come out of Africa or its people. Why should we accept the insane disparagements of our people at face value? A rhythm doesn't have to come from the black race to be good and we do not need the rhythms, nor the music, of the black race to be whole. We can instead rejoice in the rhythms natural to *us*, sing in the voices natural to *us*, and yes, dance in the manner natural to us too rather than flail our arms and contort our bodies like idiot savages which is what passes for "dancing" today. Why do we disdain ballet, the waltz, square dancing, and other forms of dancing that actually require thought and grace? When I was an adolescent, square dancing was still taught in public school. I would wager that that is no longer the case and that any appreciation of it has been replaced by ridicule. We have become divorced from our own culture at every turn. Class has been replaced by crass. White people supposedly are not "cool," not "hip" unless they forego their own nature as exhibited by their own culture. The superior has been replaced by the inferior and we lack the will to even say so. Our own culture has been abandoned, supplanted, forsaken, dispensed with in the schools and elsewhere. Actual dancing has always been both an art and a skill; what people deem as "dancing" today is neither and is rather an embarrassment. Our White people jiggle their bodies like clowns because they don't know any better. Our people have been divorced from their own culture to such an extent however that they have no sense of this; to many White people, dancing *is* what it is to the black man rather than what it was to their own ancestors. The thought, if it occurs at all, of a ballet, of a waltz, of a polka, of a square dance, or of innumerable other forms of dancing that sprang from our own people is likely to evoke derisive laughter, scorn, or dumbfounded silence. That's if our own culture comes to our minds at all. Class, grace, and talent have been discarded in favor of the primitive. Backward through the eons of time the culture of this society now finds itself. Is it not true that our youth today have more appreciation for a black Michael Jackson than for their own White Mozart? Is it not so that our true White culture stands today as a stranger to the descendants of those who created it? The minds of our White people are indeed in chains.

Even the way our White people identify *themselves* often reflects their sickness as a people. How often, for example, have we encountered White people who are obviously of that race identify themselves instead as "Native American" or "Indian" in deference to the one possible ancestor of theirs several generations back while omitting the obvious fact that the rest of their ancestors were White? In other words, rather than identify with their overwhelming White ancestry, they have so little regard for it— and conversely so *much* regard for their Indian ancestry—that they see themselves as an Indian. On the other hand, has anyone ever heard of an obvious Indian identifying himself as a White man just because one White man, several generations ago, entered his family tree? Has anyone, by the same token, heard of a black man identify himself as White because he has a fraction of White blood?

We have the situation, in other words, in which to have a small portion of Indian blood is such a great source of pride, and their overwhelming White ancestry such a source of disdain, that some White people disregard their membership in the White Race altogether. A man can be 1/16 Indian (so-called "Native American"), rejoice in that paltry 1/16, and forget about and not identify with the other 15/16 of his ancestry at all! If this is not a striking example of the lack of self-love with which our White people are afflicted, it is difficult to conceive of what would be. A man can have the blondest of hair and the bluest of eye and yet amazingly claim to belong to an Indian tribe! This is mind subversion *par excellence.* No such affliction exists in the other races though. No man of obvious black ancestry identifies himself as White just because a mere one of his sixteen great great grandparents happened to be White. No man of obvious Indian ancestry identifies himself as White because a mere one of his sixteen great great grandparents happened to be White. White people though, on the other hand, routinely do this, i.e. take what *possible* nonwhite ancestry they might have (usually unconfirmed) and identify themselves as this rather than with the ancestry that predominates within them. Why? Because their minds are in chains. There is simply no regard for being White anymore while there *is* regard for the other races. Nor is identification only at issue but so is loyalty. Our White people have thus become so demoralized that some among us don't even identify with their own race any-more, nor have any loyalty to it. To be White is a blight and so they think it away. The mind is so powerful that people can look into the mirror and negate what is there.

Nor do people seem to feel free to rejoice in their Whiteness even when they *do* embrace it: let us acknowledge the fact that if a young White man in high school were to don a t-shirt saying "White and Proud" on it, he would almost certainly face a more adverse reaction from his peers and from the school administra-tion than would be the case if a young hispanic man in high school were to don a t-shirt saying "Brown and Proud," a young black man "Black and Proud," and so forth. Any public expression of pride in being White is absolutely forbidden lest one be deemed a social outcast. The best that White people might be able to pull off without supposed "controversy" is the expression of pride in a particular nationality or ethnicity, such as Irish pride or Italian pride, but interestingly enough, the expression of pride *in the White race as a whole*—encompassing of course these nationali-ties and other nationalities of the White Race—is considered strictly off limits. In other words, we are allowed to celebrate a *branch* of the tree (our particular ethnicity) but we are oddly disal-lowed from celebrating the tree (race) itself. This is a bizarre phenomenon, is it not? The word "White" is viewed with suspi-cion, distrust, and foreboding. The minds of our White people are indeed in chains. Take a run of the mill Italian pride festival and turn it into a generalized *White* pride festival and people of all races will rebuke it, call it "racist" (which it is but for different rea-sons than understood), and there will be protests against it. In fact, is it not true that White people putting together a "White pride festival" in a major city would have a difficult time finding people even willing to attend? That either the potential White participants would be unwilling to bear the potential controversy and smears against it and them or they *themselves* would reject the notion of celebrating "White" pride? In other words, we must brood upon the fact that for every thousand White people who would be willing and happy to attend an *"Italian* pride festival," maybe only ten White people would be willing and happy to attend a "*White* pride festival" celebrating the race as a whole. Why though, as a matter of logic and common sense, should our people be favorable to the one and not the other? Why is it that many thousands of Irish-Americans happily attend St. Patrick's Day parades but would not be caught dead at a *White* pride parade? Why is it that we would be happy to enjoy Oktoberfest but would not even consider attending or holding a White Fest? The only answer is the sickness of the times and the sickness of our minds. We have been propagandized to believe that "White" is a misfortune, and thus to celebrate White people as "White" people is tantamount to holding a dance for a witch. The doors are shut, the shades pulled, and supplications made. The minds of our people are in chains.

We further have been propagandized to believe that any expression of Whiteness on our part is somehow an offense to those who are *not* White, an idea which, when reflected upon, is about as sensible as a Christian church deigning to forgo religious services for fear of "insulting" non-Christians! Why must the assertion of our very identity and pride in it be a source of insult to anyone though? And why should we let phony claims of insult defer us from rejoicing in ourselves?

We have White people today that take offense at even being *asked* whether they are proud to be White. First, they take offense at the very word "White" being uttered. Second, they take offense at the implication that they themselves are White. Third, they think that the questioner must be some kind of provocateur by virtue of asking such a question, that only an obnoxious person would *ask that*. And fourth, "proud" and "White" simply don't belong in the same sentence as far as they are concerned. It is considered less socially acceptable to ask that question than perhaps any *non*-racial question and yet the question and its answer reveal so much. Why should people take offense though at being asked whether they are proud to be *White* any more than any other form of pride? Say being asked whether you are proud to be an American, for example? If it is right to be proud to be an

American, or a Canadian, or an Australian, or whatever, why should it be wrong to be proud to be White? If it is right to be proud to be a Texan, a New Yorker, a Kentuckian, or whatever, why should it be wrong to be proud to be White? The answer of course is that it isn't. The reason why so many of our White people take offense at the straightforward question, "Are you proud to be White?" is quite simply because of the self-hatred, self-abasement, and self-derision with which our people are afflicted which this book aims to erase. There is no other answer. Only in a people that loathes itself and has been conditioned to flee from any kind of racial self-regard could the question "Are you proud to be White?" be offensive, for there is no more offense in the question any more than asking someone whether it is raining outside. *The basic assumption in our society is that White people have somehow forfeited any right, or even option, to be proud of themselves as a race* but this is an assumption without a basis that is deserved. The opening of any encyclopedia reveals plenty for White people to be proud about for again and again it is a White man or woman who contributed his or her knowledge, skill, passion, and yes, genius to this world. If your father, cousins, and brothers were to accomplish much in their lives, would you not be proud of them? Why then should it be any different as to our race as a whole whose accomplishments throughout history are not only innumerable but are without parallel, to the objective observer, in any other race? If each of us had a brother who had invented electric lighting, the automobile, the computer, the transistor, and thousands of other inventions, would we not be proud of him? Why then should we not be proud to be members of a race that invented all of these things? On the other hand, if we shouldn't be proud to be White because obviously not all White people are saints or even good people, then on that basis we shouldn't be proud to be Americans, Canadians, or Australians either, should we? As always, the positive identification and attribution to matters concerning country, but negative identification and attribution when it comes to the White Race, makes no logical sense. If the first is good, the second must be good as well but actually the second is far more valid than the first. People everywhere are expected to pronounce a pride in their country but White people everywhere are expected to *de*nounce a pride in their race. Our minds are indeed in chains.

It may be argued that some of the discomfort with the notion of White people, White pride, a White Race stems from an actual awareness of strength, of being in power and thus having no need to embrace such things, that we are a majority so why think or care about Whiteness at all? This though only begs the question: why should a people *ever* choose not to embrace itself? Why should its feeling of self-worth be dependent on its having *little* power? Should not our White people instead love itself regardless of its material circumstances and regardless of its numbers? Furthermore, White people who either consciously or subconsciously rest their thoughts and actions upon a White majority status (in America) may well wake up one day to find that they are no longer a majority at all, largely due to their very lack of White self-love and loyalty today. If what is really at issue here were the bashfulness of the supposedly stronger (White) versus the supposedly weaker (non-white), White people would do well to realize that their Race is a pitifully small percentage of the world's population (1/14 today), is rapidly shrinking percentage-wise in the United States and in our own European ancestral homeland, and that whatever material, economic advantage we currently have is consistently decreasing in favor of non-whites within our own countries and abroad in India, China, and so forth. If we wish to reverse the trend of our dispossession as a Race, we would also do well to cease being shamed out of looking out for our own best interests as this is the only way that our dispossession can be thwarted. With a White Race unwilling to lift a finger in its own defense, we can hardly expect the other races to do that for us and nor will they. We can hardly expect help from others when we are unwilling to help ourselves. No. Our dispossession can only be thwarted through the assertion of our own will.

Our White people today though are not even nearly at the point at which they would realize or even care about such a dispossession, for one can only be wary about one's dispossession as a people so long as one first possesses an *identity* as that people. We today no longer have that identity. We are instead atomized "individuals" whose being is encouraged from all quarters to begin and end with our own individual selves. Have you noticed that the other races are thought of as groups while only *White* people are thought of as individuals? Blacks in America were expected, for example, to vote for the half-black candidate for president en masse (and they dutifully did so) whereas White people as "individuals" were expected to divide their votes between the two candidates and hence neutralize the voting bloc that *they* could possess. Blacks could freely announce that they were going to vote for Barack Obama because he was "black" but in no wise was it remotely deemed socially acceptable for White people to vote for John McCain because he was White. That would be "racist," after all! In reality though, one is not any more racist than the other and if tens of millions of blacks voted for Barack Obama because he was black and were morally justified for it, White people would have been just as morally justified to vote for John McCain en masse because he was White. Of course, they didn't, however. Instead, as usual, our votes *canceled each other out*. Amazingly, the largest racial population in America does not even have a voting bloc! Is it not true that a group mentality is encouraged when the group in question is non-white, only to be discouraged when the group in question is White? Again, this is a strange sort of "equality": only White people are expected and urged to be "colorblind" while the other races are expected and urged to see color to their hearts' content. Obviously the "National Association for the Advancement of *Colored* People" is not "colorblind," for example, and so why should White people be so? Why should we alone embrace what is, after all, a genetic *defect* in Nature, a genetic defect that, by the way, greatly decreases an organism's chance for survival? To not see color is to not see the real world and to not see the real world is to likely fall prey to it. The NAACP sees color, the color of its own people, but we White people do in fact have our *own* color too: our *White* color that deserves as much "advancement" as any else. To not see color, to be "color-blind," is to be a *victim* and indeed our beloved colorblind White people are the victims of today, a people enslaved by its own confused thinking, a people whose mind is in chains. We actually *do* see color when it comes to lifting up and otherwise assisting the other races but when it comes to looking out for the best interests, or even *any* interests of our own people for that matter, we are indeed "blind."

Anyone in a moment of honesty and reflection—and with some courage as well—will admit that all men are *not* created equal and that this inequality exists everywhere both within races and between races. The idea that all men emerge from the womb with equal potential or abilities is so blatantly false that no one feels it necessary to refute such a thing. Why then do we accept the mantra of "equality" like some kind of holy writ? Why must we then deceive ourselves and our children? Why do we lie and say that everyone can become a rocket scientist, that everyone can become president, that everyone, if he or she "only works hard enough," can accomplish anything that he or she desires? Gaze upon a racetrack and tell me that all men are created equal. Show me a child with birth defects and tell me that all men are created equal; to have less or more than others in any respect refutes the idea of equality on its face. Men are not matchsticks, all of equal length and equal design. Rather, there is variety and variety itself means inequality (non-sameness). Not everyone can become a Mozart or Michelangelo regardless of upbringing because the raw material is simply not there. And thank goodness this is true! What a lack of worthwhile world it would be if we were all the same (i.e. equal), all with the same physical abilities, all with the same mental capacities, all with the same desires, all with the same character. If we were all created equal, the distinction between good and bad men could not exist. Every man would be interchangeable with every other, every potential wife or husband would be interchangeable with every other, every child would be interchangeable with every other. Who on earth really believes that this is so? Every single mark of distinction in this world is a mark of inequality and it is this distinction, this ine-quality that makes human life even possible. Otherwise we would be mere herd animals on a field but even there, there is the stronger and the weaker, the faster and the slower, and the taller and the shorter (i.e. the unequal).

Again, there can be no equality of man because all men are not the same and indeed, the higher the form of life in general, the less equality there is. Two rabbits, for example, which are well-nigh indistinguishable from one another, may be to all in-tents and purposes "equal" to one another but this is clearly not so in the case of man whose individuals *are* distinguishable from one another. Rabbits do not reason, rabbits do not talk, and rab-bits look alike, those factors and others increasing the equality among them. None of this though is true with man. In other words, the more variety, the more that inequality exists. This is not to say that one must then always make a judgment as to which being is better, or superior to the other, but it does mean that "equality," when it comes to man himself, is a concept with-out meaning and devoid of value. It also means, critically, that all attempts to make the *races* of man equal to one another in their lives, based on this inherent "equality," are foolhardy, and if the races of man are not in fact equal to one another, where is the justification for all of the foreign and domestic policies based on that alleged equality? Why should White people ever make way for the non-white races in any respect due to their alleged "equal-ity" when they are not, in fact, our equals? Thus all racial egalitar-ianism has a foundation built of sand. Individuals are not equal to one another and races are not equal to one another. Since races are not equal to one another, policies based on the notion that they are must be inherently flawed. Granting that individuals are not equal to one another (are not the same as one another), rac-es, which are composed of individuals, cannot be equal to one another either. The whole dogma thus falls apart. The mania for alleged "equality" is just that: mania. The past one hundred years in that regard have been about as sensible as debating how many angels can dance upon the head of a pin as monks did in the Middle Ages. People sadly have always been zealous in their pursuit of phantoms. The reason why "equality" has become such a sacred cow for us is simply because its promotion is habitual. Habit becomes tradition and tradition becomes second-nature. If you are uncomfortable and even offended that I have challenged the notion of "equality," stop and consider whether that in itself makes me wrong or whether instead the discomfort and offense you feel is really simply a reflex reaction to what you in your life have always been told is a good. The problem though is that the supposed "good" of equality has never been examined, analyzed, or dissected but when it is, we find in our hand a mere vanishing mote of a sunbeam rather than the diamond that has, for so long, been claimed and presumed to be the case.

There are far more broad differences among men than among any other races of life except perhaps dogs whose races (breeds) were crafted by men through selective breeding. There are more differences among men in intelligence, physical strength, personality, and essential character than among any other form of life whether it be bees, bears, or bobcats. Two bears are far more alike (equal) than two men. Thus the idea of equality is, ironically enough, even *more* untrue of the only beings who are capable of even conceiving of such a notion—men—than it is of any other form of life. In other words, a bear doesn't have any notion of equality and yet equality is far more applicable to his kind than to man's which does. Put still another way, bears cannot conceive of "equality" even though they are at least *nearly* equal to one another while men *can* conceive of "equality" even though they aren't *even close* to being equal to one another. This is indeed a great irony: the only races of life on earth that can even dream up an idea of equality of their members are the ones whose members are the *least* equal to one another. There is far more uniqueness among men (inequality) than among any other forms of life on earth. One would be hard pressed to detect distinctions (inequalities) between two mice of the same breed but distinctions (inequalities) between two men of the same breed, or different breeds of course, are too numerous to count! Thus, rather than any supposed equality of man, there is *distinction*. This distinction is what typifies man. Some men are geniuses and some men are brutes. They are unequal because they are not the same. If you are looking to solve a mathematical formula, you might consider the genius to be superior for that purpose. On the other hand, if you are in need of "brute strength" to haul some concrete blocks, you might consider the brute to be superior for *that* purpose, and indeed, you would be a fool if you were to pay no mind to these differences between the two men, instead preferring to think of them as "equal" to one another. Thus it is the notion of "equality" that is objectively false while the notions of superiority and inferiority are subjectively true since they are based on point of view and function.

Needless to say, the society of today has these matters backwards. Distinction, difference, and variety exist everywhere and hence notions of superiority (meaning "higher") and inferiority (meaning "lower") naturally come into play constantly even if people mistakenly often have misgivings concerning usage of those particular words. Our taste buds may tell us that this apple is superior to that apple and thus that apple is inferior to this one. In matters of taste such as this example, we are most willing to use the words superior and inferior to connote that which we prefer but why should it be any different when it comes to men? I have met some superior men in my life and I have met many inferior ones. This is my judgment and my taste. Since all men are not equal, created as such or otherwise, no one will have the same exact judgment and taste and nor does he or she *need* to. Even Martin Luther King, as enamored as he was with the concept of "equality," recognized that there was such a thing as a superior character and thus allowed for people to be judged by that. All the while though, he was engaged at improving things for his *race*, notably enough, but whether it ever occurred to him that White people doing the same for *their* race must necessarily *oppose* his efforts is anyone's guess.

I may though be getting ahead of myself. Since there is no equality (sameness) in men, we are left with difference, distinction, variety, inequality, and, ultimately, *preference and interest.* When it comes to the races of men, we naturally prefer *those who are like us*; in other words, *those of our own kind* just as does every other race on earth. A grizzly bear prefers the company of other grizzly bears, not that of black bears. Sparrows prefer the company of other sparrows, not cardinals or crows. Grizzly bears and black bears are both "bears" but they are not the same (equal), are different in character and physicality, are distinctive in appearance, and hence they do not intermingle nor of course interbreed in any way. Does any well-meaning person ever try to claim or pronounce that the two kinds of bears are "equal" to one another? Why then should people be so quick to pronounce that the two races of *men*, say White and black, are equal to one another? Indeed, the very fact that we are dealing with two *different* races, whether of men or of bears, proves that they are not equal—the *same*—as one another. If bears could reason and speak, would they really have any use for this "equality" business? Only in men, the only creatures on earth capable of abstract thought regardless of the truth or falsity of the particular idea in question, does such an abstract notion devoid of any fact unfortunately assume the role of an idol. Does anyone ever insist that grizzly bears and black bears "integrate"? No, because their preference and their interest dictate otherwise and, of course, nobody ever wasted his time on proclaiming them "equal" in the first place or worth the special attention that we devote to men. Rather, a grizzly bear naturally prefers his own kind and this naturality makes it right. Can you imagine how incredulous these respective bears would be if you could somehow communicate to them that they should "integrate"? One might expect them to say "Hey, we're not the same!"

One would hope that White people would be acknowledged to have at least as much prerogative as bears and other forms of life to follow Nature's Laws and prefer their own kind and seek their own interests. In other words, is it really right to deny our White Race that which is naturally possessed by every other creature on this earth? Every creature naturally looks out for its own kind, pursuing its own interests without regard to the preferences or interests of other kinds. This is the way that they maintain their existence as unique, *diverse* forms of life. Everywhere in Nature there is racial exclusiveness for if there were not, no races would exist. Thus ironically, those who struggle the most for alleged "diversity" in society are actually doing the most to destroy true diversity in man, for mixing the races of man socially, sexually, and environmentally destroys, obliterates the very diversity these people say they love so much. Only through separation can each race retain its true character.

Let me make the point more clear: when different races are brought together within the same society, they inevitably assimilate with one another as well as amalgamate (interbreed). They are expected to follow a common morality, a common culture, a common language, and have the same or at least similar attitudes. This though is the *antithesis* of diversity. The distinctions (i.e. diversity) in man are broken down through this institution of commonality. In America it is sometimes mused that one day the races will be so interbred that the races will no longer be distinguishable. Well, if the day comes when there are no longer distinctive races of men but rather one big mongrelized so-called "human" race, how can it be said that there will still be diversity? With the existence of White people, black people, yellow people, and brown people, there is diversity. To mix (mongrelize) them together, there is not. With thousands of languages in the world, there is diversity of tongue; if everybody on the contrary only spoke one language, there would not be diversity of tongue. Diversity is thus best maintained by keeping the differences in man intact, by *rejecting* "equality," by *rejecting* integration, by *rejecting* amalgamation, and by *rejecting* assimilation. Those who, on the contrary, have fought for such policies while at the same time trumpeting "diversity," have sacrificed long-term reality for short-term misplaced desires. True, *society* is more "diverse" when it is multi-racial (hetero-geneous) rather than mono-racial (homogeneous) but the diversity of man *himself* is destroyed in the process, perhaps irrevocably. As with "equality" though, people neglect to really scrutinize what diversity means and what it doesn't. The words are never really reflected upon but are rather usually used to *replace* thought. It is always assumed, for example, that the white separatist is against diversity when in reality the white separatist, black separatist, brown separatist, et cetera are the most dedicated to maintaining it. The very notion of a melting pot, so routinely uttered without reflection, illustrates the contradiction between assimilation and diversity, for melting various foods together in a pot obviously destroys their distinct nature, their distinct taste, their *diversity*. Everything starts to taste indistinguishably. That is largely the point of cooking but do we really wish to "cook" men? Do we really wish to meld (assimilate) them together, eliminating their uniqueness? Do we really wish to be a one size fits all conglomerate, adapted to the demands of the artificial society that we have crafted for ourselves, instead of having a society adapted *to us as we are* as it should be? This is, and would be, the degradation of man.

We as White people should not be forced to adapt ourselves to society; we have the right and prerogative to force society to adapt to *us*, to fulfill *our* needs as a race, to advance *our* culture, to protect *our* genes. Nor was America of course founded as a "melting pot" in the first place. Rather, this notion has been foisted upon us by the duplicitous and the ignorant to justify the incessant waves of non-white immigrants into what was once *our* country alone. It is also said that we are a "nation of immigrants" but this doesn't mean that we ever had to be a "nation" of *all* immigrants from everywhere in the world. Our country is supposed to be our home but who ever heard of a homeowner being forced to open his home to anyone who wants to enter? No, he *discriminates* as he should and we as White Americans had and have a right to discriminate as to the racial characteristics of those seeking to enter our home, our country. Equality of immigration rights and freedom practically contradict one another, for forcing a people to grant all men the right to enter America regardless of race takes away the freedom of White people to live with whom they choose, the freedom of White people to have the country of their own desire. Why should we make way, bow down in deference to the supposed rights of others when our own rights are sacrificed in the process? Especially when the temporary diversification of our *society* leads to the destruction of diversity in *man*?

Incidentally, the claim that all men are equal is in effect a *repudiation* of diversity, for if men were truly equal (the same), they could not also be diverse (not the same). How many people though erroneously think that "equality" and "diversity" go hand in hand! This is one of the marvels of our times.

Rather than "equality," the guiding light for all creatures at all times is *interest*. What is in our best interests? What is in the best interests of this or that race? Peel away Martin Luther King's campaign for "equal rights" and you will realize that it was merely a *means* to an end, not an end in itself. The end, rather, was the furtherance of the best interests, as he saw them, *of black people*. Whether or not he truly believed that all men are equal as he preached, he viewed a struggle by blacks for equal rights and their successful acquisition *as being in the best interests of his race*. As a black man, these were the only interests under his consideration in the campaign; never were the best interests of White people, on the other hand, at issue at all, rightly enough, *since the man wasn't White*.

This is not to say that Martin Luther King was *right* that his struggle furthered the best interests of his own race, only that this was the purpose of his struggle. He came to the conclusion that equal legal rights for blacks were good for blacks. On the other hand, if he had come to the conclusion that equal legal rights for blacks (as he characterized them, of course) were *bad* for blacks, he would not have engaged in his struggle. He thought that racial integration was good for blacks; Malcolm X thought that racial integration was bad for blacks. The common denominator for both men, as well as other historical black leaders such as Frederick Douglass, Booker T. Washington, Marcus Garvey, and W.E.B. Dubois was *what was best for blacks*. The question as to what was best for White people wasn't even in the room, let alone on the table. People indeed would have thought it strange, if not downright idiotic, if any of these men would have ever found themselves chastised for not properly considering the best interests of *White* people in their endeavors! And yet amazingly, *White* people aren't supposed to consider the best interests of White people either! Yes, the minds of our White people are in chains.

Indeed, somehow during the 1960's, the best interests of White people were totally subsumed by the struggle for the best interests of black people. When blacks (and their multitude of White helpers) sought to increase the power of blacks by registering them to vote, nobody seemed to reflect upon the fact that the power of *Whites* would be diminished thereby. When blacks (and their multitude of White helpers) sought to integrate the public schools under the notion that blacks would obtain a better education if they were educated alongside White people, nobody seemed to reflect that there was a distinct if not high possibility that White people would obtain a *worse* education by being educated alongside blacks, which has indeed been strongly borne out by the education statistics the past forty years (the more White students are integrated with blacks in school, the worse the educational performance of those students on average. Indeed, the downfall of the American educational system versus that of the rest of the world is directly attributable to Whites being forced to integrate with non-whites in the schools and the massive growth of the non-white population in the country itself.). Martin Luther King was spared from being called a racist simply because he fought for what he deemed were the best interests of *black* people. If, on the other hand, he had fought for what he deemed were the best interests of *White* people and were indeed a *White* man, the label (wrongly understood of course) would have been applied to him galore. Such is the bizarre hypocrisy, or double-standard, that puts the minds of our White people in chains. The same logic that would put one race at the Lincoln Memorial by the thousands (the furtherance of black interests) is denied altogether to another race, ours (the furtherance of White interests).

It is an unacknowledged fact that the White men, women,

and children who protested the integration of their schools were fighting for their race just as rightly as the blacks trying to integrate them and yet their having done so makes them today an object of reproach—rather than admiration as in the case with the blacks—due to the confused state of mind our White people suffer today. Is it right to condemn our own people for asserting their own best interests while at the same time applauding blacks for asserting theirs? The difference though was that the blacks were trying to invade that which had belonged to another race while the Whites were merely trying to stop such an invasion from occurring. Under normal circumstances, one would thus think that the moral and ethical high ground was held *by the Whites*. Indeed, objectively speaking, do we usually root for the invader or for the defender? Do we usually root for the home invader or for the home owner? If someone wants to take up residence in your house tomorrow, don't you think that you should be able to say no?

The problem, as always, is White self-denial. We would deny to our own people schools of their own and yet we would never even think about denying blacks schools of *their* own. We would support the integration of White neighborhoods but spare black neighborhoods any such integration. We would forbear ourselves while prodding the other races to *assert* themselves. We would assume that any professed grievances on the part of non-whites are just but that any professed grievances on the part of Whites are *un*just. Hence the champion of blacks, Martin Luther King, has a nearly god-like reputation while champions of Whites are scourged. He is the only American whose birthday is a federal holiday, his image (graven image?) appears on a postage stamp, and a memorial to him on par with that of Lincoln or Jefferson (or even bigger?) is currently being built in the federal capital. All the while, memorials to any champion of White people, *our* people, are ruthlessly torn down wherever they appear or are squelched in their cradle. Do you not see how thoroughly our minds have been in chains? And is it not the case that even when we are conscious of the double-standard and the wrong that has been done to our White people these years that we *still* forbear ourselves? Indeed, many of us know that we've been wronged and yet we *pretend* that that is not the case. How many thousands or millions of people don't think that there should be any holiday to King, for example, and yet how *few* are willing to say so? So much has been forced down our throats; so few of us have had the will to say "thanks, but no thanks." We are told that we have "freedom of speech" but it is implicitly understood that that does not include saying nay to black furtherance (at our expense) and the idolization and indeed near worship of their champion. (What White public figure feels free to denounce the King holiday?) The White Christian has two gods, Jesus Christ and Martin Luther King, whether he would want them or not. If I am wrong then let the King holiday ("holy day") be revoked. The fervor by which it is clung to speaks for itself.

Much has been made about King's commitment to non-violence but this too, like the struggle for (allegedly) equal rights for blacks, was merely a *means* to an end rather than an end itself: the furtherance of black interests. Simply put, if King had thought that violence would advance the best interests of his race better than non-violence, he would have chosen violence. Instead, he was shrewd enough to know that a violent movement of blacks against Whites would, unlike a peaceful movement, mobilize Whites *en masse* against it and his entire program. The most sympathetic White liberals—upon whom his movement largely relied—would have fled for cover and the much-condemned Ku Klux Klan, in opposition to such a violent movement, would instead have been regarded as heroes, literally rescuing White knights, rather than terrorists. Wear the clothing of a sheep regardless of whether you are a sheep or a wolf, as it were. White people are willing to put up with much but mass violence is where they draw the line. King, a student of Gandhi, knew that his trump card was *the* (misplaced) *compassion of White people*. To allow violence to be done to you without fighting back—as King's movement practiced—evokes *compassion* but to fight violence with violence evokes fear, alarm, and ultimately leads to more violence because people eventually forget, or no longer care, who committed the violence first. Thus, if King's minions had fought back in the streets or at the lunch counters or elsewhere against the violence perpetrated against them, they would ultimately have appeared to be more like aggressors in the eyes of the White masses and thus they would have lost the support of mainstream America. Hence King instructed his minions to reject both offensive violence as well as defensive violence (self-defense) because both forms of violence would hurt their cause. The record is quite clear on this point. The so-called "civil rights movement," as it styled itself, did not forgo violence out of some kind of moral superiority, love for White "oppresssors," or because it violated the participants' principles, but rather because it was simply the best, and indeed the only winnable, tactic for the time and the circumstances in which they found themselves. It was willing to suffer in order to win and indeed, King deliberately *sought out* the infliction of suffering upon his adherents as a means of supposedly showing White people that his cause was just and that of the status quo unjust. The tactic of non-violence was born of weakness, not strength. Being outnumbered in the country at least eight to one, a violent black "civil rights movement," so-called, would have brought down nearly the entire White populace against it but a *non*-violent movement was instead able to pull on the Christian heartstrings of the Whites and convince many of them that they had nothing to fear by the success of such a movement.

Sympathy (compassion) is indeed a powerful emotion in people regardless of whether we view it as good or bad. The so-called "civil rights movement" could not hope to win its professed aims without garnering the support of a significant number of Whites and sympathy was the best, and maybe the only, way to do it. Which evokes more sympathy for demonstrators, images of them *shooting* at police dogs or images of them being *attacked* by them? There is something in man today that disdains perceived victimization, a tendency to root for the weak against the brutality of the strong and to have compassion for them regardless of whether the cause they represent is just on the merits or not.

Christian teaching, of course, buttressed (or even caused) this sentiment as King knew full well. Thus he formed his Southern *Christian* Leadership Conference and otherwise went about his struggle through religious trappings and religious dogma on behalf of the "oppressed" which could not help but resonate well in a Christian society. Never mind the fact that it was their very White "oppressors" who had introduced Christianity to blacks in the first place! The irony is indeed thick: the religion that was used in one era as a means of keeping blacks content with their enslaved condition ("Blessed are the meek," et cetera) could be used in another era as a means to overthrow the dominant White society on alleged grounds of "inequality." Christianity is, to be sure, capable of different interpretations; thus during one era it was held to endorse the maintaining of Negro slavery and yet during another era it was held to somehow demand full "civil rights" for the descendants of the slaves in American society. There are some Christians who still believe that the latter is indeed a true Christian teaching though in my own reading of The Bible, I have never been able to find a single verse that supports that and certainly not through lack of trying. As for passages supporting the institution of slavery, on the other hand, we do find this, among others: "Slaves, obey your earthly masters with respect and fear, and with sincerity of heart, just as you would obey Christ." Ephesians 6:5 Nowhere in The Bible, incidentally, does it ever say that all men, or the races of men, are equal, are created that way or otherwise, nor that the races should integrate in any society or share the same (equal) status in that society. Historically and for our purposes though, what matters is not what Christianity actually teaches but rather what people think it teaches or would *want* it to teach. Further, if a movement styles itself as being Christian and claims to be struggling for Christian principles, it will usually be accepted as such, at least by many people. In the hustle and bustle of daily life, few have the opportunity or inclination to really investigate the claims of those around them; it is easier to simply take them at their word.

To this day, many White people are confused by the non-violent *tactic* into thinking that the *cause* must be just when in reality there is a world of difference between the two. So what if a cause uses peaceful means? That merely indicates that the advocates for it think that their cause is better served thereby. A cause is not made even an ounce more just because it forsakes violence as a tactic since a tactic is a mere means to an end while a cause is the end in itself. Thus the so-called "civil rights movement" merely used the tactic that would enable it to prevail, its pacifism in the face of violence being unfortunately mistaken by the Whites for righteousness. An act of willpower (in not fighting back against the violence inflicted upon you) is simply not the same as demonstrating that one's cause is itself just. This distinction though was too subtle for a White people who, for the first time, had been exposed to a television media culture and they could not grasp it. Whites saw blacks being beaten on their living room television sets and their emotions were stirred. Without this new invention of television, this obviously would not have happened. A sympathy was stirred through the visual exercise of brutality that could never have been stirred without that visualization being inches away from them on their television screens. Our people gradually became convinced that the cause of the so-called "civil rights movement" must be just because surely the participants wouldn't go through so much hell for it if it weren't? By the same reasoning though we would have to declare the cause of the communist North Vietnamese against America in the Vietnam War just too since they too went through hell and so have other causes throughout history. Mere sacrifice thus proves nothing.

I have said that a non-violent tactic does not make a particular cause just, and this is the case no matter how much violence is perpetrated against those who espouse it. Conversely though, and perhaps even more importantly, the use of violence *by* those espousing a particular cause does not, in itself, make that cause *un*just, and this fact too was sadly overlooked and missed by our people in the 1950's and 1960's and has been to this day as well. The sentiment was (and is) as follows: "violence is being perpetrated against the peaceful 'civil rights' workers and so the cause in opposition to them must be bad" but this isn't any more true than that the cause of the so-called "civil rights workers" was good because they *didn't* use violence. This is an important point because our people have been quite simply transfixed by the fact that one side employed considerable violence and the other didn't as if that somehow settled the matter as to who was right and who was wrong. *It didn't because a tactic is just that, a tactic.* One side employed violence and the other didn't. So what? That just means that the one thought that violence would enable it best to prevail and the other that it wouldn't. The White people who violently resisted the efforts to dispossess them of what was theirs did so in that manner simply because they possessed the *strength* to do so; the "civil rights movement" did *not* employ violence simply because it was *too weak* to do so and because such means would have been counter-productive. Hence the means do not justify the ends nor condemn them. By means of analogy, there would never have been United States of America without violence but does that mean that the founding of the Union was wrong? Conversely, pederasts, flat-earthers, and end of the world prophets all promote their respective causes through non-violence but does that make their causes right? Not hardly.

The so-called "civil rights movement" simply practiced a form of psychological warfare as most, if not all, movements do. It insinuated first of course that it was fighting for supposed "rights" by its usage of the "civil rights" moniker and this immediately lulled people into thinking that blacks had "rights" that were being denied. It's as if a baseball team were to name itself "The Best Team"; automatically people are going to assume that it is indeed the best team by virtue of the mere usage of the name. In other words, call something a "right" and you tend to immediately have people trying to vindicate that "right" with not much time being spent on reflecting upon whether the "right" actually exists. People take the fictitious claim totally at face value, being duped by a well-chosen propaganda term and nothing more. The "right" is assumed and it is assumed with great indignation. By repeatedly styling itself as a "civil rights movement," people were conditioned into believing that it was truly fighting for things that its adherents were entitled to whereas, in reality, no such "rights" existed and do not, in fact, exist today. For decades, our minds as White people have been in a straitjacket with us under the impression that if we seek anything at all in our own interests as a people, we are infringing on the "civil rights" of non-whites when in reality, the term "civil rights" was just a propaganda term all along. When though the so-called "civil rights movement" *did* reference some kind of source for their alleged (and usually simply assumed) "rights," it was usually the hazy notion of "human rights" or, worse still, the Declaration of Independence which had nothing to do obviously with the "civil rights" of blacks since it was written, endorsed, and subscribed by slaveholders. More important though is the inherent contradiction in the fact that a professed "civil rights movement" found it necessary to fight for "civil rights" *legislation*. In other words, if what it was really fighting for was the "rights" of black people, *no legislation would have been necessary since these rights were supposed to have already existed*. Still in other words, if the law did not already provide the "rights," *the "rights" did not actually exist* and hence why the campaigners pushed for the enactment of *new* laws so that the "rights" would now exist. Thus the very campaign for "civil rights legislation" tacitly admitted that no rights had previously been at issue or violated since they would actually come into existence only once the new legislation was passed. (Even so, the "rights" *still* do not exist since the legislation in question violates the Constitution of the United States.)

Thus, in reality, what was being fought for was *new* rights, not the vindication of old ones. Thus it was not that blacks in America were denied their "rights" so much as they wanted *new* ones which again, as stated earlier, automatically decreased those of Whites. There is simply no such thing as increasing the power of one group in society without decreasing the power of another. This is a truism that is unfortunately almost universally ignored but by means of analogy, isn't it a fact that the bigger the portion of pie given to one group, the smaller that remains for the other? When reflected upon, "rights" is really just another word for *power* and the *increase* of one group's power (rights) means the *decrease* of another's. Power is in every society a zero-sum gain. This is easily illustrated by the example provided by the 1964 "civil rights" act itself whereby, among other things, the newly provided legal right of blacks to be served in restaurants owned by Whites, or housed in hotels owned by Whites, gave them such a power while taking away the power of the White owners to serve and house whom they chose. It is always assumed that the power of White people is somehow constant, that the so-called "civil rights movement" did not take anything away from us, that the White people who resisted it were wrong for not wanting to generously dispense "rights" to the blacks because they as White people had nothing to lose in the process. This is false on numerous levels and yet it has saturated our thinking as a people for decades. The legacy of the so-called "civil rights movement" for our White people is, in fact, nothing other than massive crime against our people by black perpetrators, the destruction of the educational system due to racial integration, the nigrification of our White culture, amalgamation (racial interbreeding), and the self-hatred and mental slavery of our race which I have sought in my limited, but hopeful way to combat with this book. The danger, if not insurmountable hurdle, is that the minds of our people have been enchained by false concepts for so long that they will be unable to extricate themselves from them. Though it is often said that truth wins out in the end, nobody can really know that since nobody has ever experienced such an "end." Time simply continues on unabated and thus no "end" is ever reached.

The bottom line about the professed civil rights movement is that it was dedicated to and propagated for the best interests of blacks alone. It had nothing to do with the best interests of our White people. Indeed, White people were called upon to *sacrifice* their best interests and in fact did so, and we are expected to continue sacrificing those best interests to this day. White people are expected to jump whenever a Negro cries "Boo!" It is considered socially acceptable for blacks to criticize Whites but considered socially unacceptable for Whites to criticize blacks. If blacks are better athletes, they did it through hard work. If Whites are better thinkers, it is because they are "privileged" and have "held blacks down." In reality, Martin Luther King was a black racist because he fought for what he deemed to be in the best interests of black people. Nobody should begrudge him that, only chastise ourselves as White people for failing to fight for the best interests of *our* people. If black people wish to make him their saint then let them do so but we as White people need our own saints and they certainly should not be composed of those of another race who fought for that race at the expense of our own. If King was a savior of the black man, that doesn't mean he was a savior of the White man. *Fighting for alleged "equality" is no more virtuous than fighting for aggrandizement* as both are simply a means to an end: in the case of King and his professed civil rights movement, the best interests of *black* people. They wanted to be "equal" with us but that doesn't mean that we should want to be "equal" with them. They said that we owed them but we did not have to agree. Instead we should have had our own path and a recognition of and an allegiance to our own best interests.

No creature on earth, past or present, has ever been as willing to sacrifice its own best interests as has our White people. Indeed, we are now practically programmed to not even *consider* those best interests after decades of media, government, and classroom propaganda. Indeed, with a White people that is today unwilling, and perhaps even unable, to conceive that it has a separate, unique, and important independent existence, how can it conceive that it has "best interests" to protect at all? The entire "mainstream" political system does not include a single voice speaking up for those interests and yet King has been made into some kind of god for fighting for the best interests of *black* people. Do you not perceive the double-standard, my White Brother or Sister? Indeed, the sheer craziness of our times? Can we indeed come to realize and recognize that we are, indeed, Brothers and Sisters of a racial family that deserves to exist and thrive for itself as much as the others do for themselves? That it is *our* interests that should matter to us, not the interests of every race *but* us? To cede power (so-called "rights") to another race is to sacrifice the power/rights of your own race, to, in effect, betray your own race. Is it good though to be traitors to your own people?

We see a (further) striking example of this self-treachery in the hideous case of South Africa whereby the White people there actually voted to give the heavy black majority the vote, thus eliminating their own power there forevermore under such a system. (This sacrifice of White political power of course came after decades of economic and political pressure from their fellow *White* people from around the world.) Nelson Mandela, a convicted terrorist who was actually guilty of terrorist acts by his own admission, to top it all off became, *in the eyes of the White people*, a hero with White political leaders and celebrities from around the world fawning all over him. With little thought actually given to the matter, Mandela was and is considered a hero by Whites for fighting for *black* people whereas these same Whites condemned those White leaders in South Africa who fought for *White* people. Apparently a black terrorist gets a free pass if he commits his terrorism in an effort to further his own race while White people who seek to further their own race *without* any terrorism deserve condemnation by these same White people. Can you not discern the mental sickness that has come over our people? White people would rather castigate their own kind as oppressors than care one whit about their own best interests. No one could possibly have believed that the best interests of the *White* people of South Africa were going to be served by surrendering their power to the black majority and yet the White people there—by majority vote at least—did it anyway. (Again, the concern of White people was what might be good for *black* people, or at least a concern for raceless "democracy," with concern for White people being totally ignored.) They did it after years of worldwide *White* propaganda against White rule, essentially a fixation of White people upon suicide. No outside enemy could have ever beaten us and so we have insisted upon beating ourselves. Instead of circling the wagons to protect our kind as we did as a people in the 19th century, in the 20th and 21st centuries we have joined with the redskins to shoot at them! White people have duped themselves into thinking that they somehow have a duty to put their arms around the shoulders of Jerome and Josè and extol their position, their viewpoint, and their interests against that of their own John and Jennifer and they have no sense of how insane that truly is. They have come to believe that power is bad whenever it is associated with Whites and yet on the other hand good when associated with non-whites. Why though should power be a good thing for one group and not for another?

Let it be clearly stated though that the matter is not, and never has been, about hating or disliking non-whites but rather that White people should not hate or dislike *themselves*. Thus the propaganda that has attacked any sense of White self-love has always wrongly labeled that self-love as "hate" when the reality is that the true hatred actually rests with those White people who do not care about the continued existence of White people as a people. In other words, amazingly enough, White people are smeared as "haters" for daring to love their own race but it is the White people who do the smearing who are actually motivated by hate even if that hate is so deeply within their subconscious that they do not recognize it. This was intimated earlier but let it be explicit. Now, after generations of this mind subversion, attacking White loyalists as "haters" has become almost second nature, routine, and automatic without giving any thought to what is really at issue. It would seem that the White man is not even entitled to have his own personal feelings anymore, that Big Brother (or Big Sister!) is always looking over his shoulder and trying to snatch any thoughts of his that may indicate "prejudice," "bigotry," or "intolerance" on his part. Every White man in his employment, and every White man especially on television, knows that if he dares say anything that could violate the societal dogma of White self-immolation, he faces almost certain firing or worse. Thus our White people are trained to think that such thoughts are bad, indeed reprehensible, when they are not, for we are psychologically predisposed to believe that only that which is bad is subject to being punished. In other words, if caring about the future of White people as White people *weren't* bad, why would people face punishment (persecution) for expressing thoughts along those lines? Through repeated "examples" being made of anyone who expresses any White loyalist feelings (firing, arrest, verbal condemnation, etc.), our people are deluded into believing that White Loyalty is wrong the same way that societal oppression determined what was deemed right and wrong in George Orwell's *1984*. Through the repetition of persecutions, the true oppression of our White people is systematized in our minds with only the rare individual giving it a second thought, for this would require an independent mode of thinking that is precisely a casualty of the current societal oppression. In other words, the more that all forms and expressions of White identity are rebuked by those wielding power and influence, and the longer this occurs, the more suppressed does White identity become within our minds and indeed, the more 'righteously' we run headlong to our own suicide as a people. Hostility to our own White people becomes so entrenched that we do not recognize it for what it is. Without even a pause, we consequently attack anything favorable to White identity instantaneously and never afterwards even reflect upon whether the attack was just. How often I have witnessed this I cannot count because it is so endemic. Why though should any belief in this world be assumed to be right or wrong without even a scintilla of analysis? Where is the debate? Where is the dialogue? The notion that there are ideas in this world so "self-evidently" wrong so as to justify their removal from any kind of contemplation and conversation—such as White identity, White loyalty, and White advocacy—is in reality simply an admission that your mind is in chains, that as free as you think you are, you are really a slave. You have let others form for you the rules of your own mind. Your thoughts and actions follow a script not of your own making. The individual who looks upon himself as among the most open minded actually has his (or her, of course) brain in a box. Among our youth, only insatiable energy—and the natural urge to rebel against that which was set in stone without their involvement—enables them to more potentially break the chains encompassing their minds. We can hope that they may not let us down in that regard! May the youth in their natural rebellion be willing to pick up the hammer and wield it with force upon the chisel resting upon the chains of their mental enslavement— and even if pain may necessarily be involved!

The open mind is not just what the television set, the politicians, and "society" tells you it is and it is within your power to issue a resounding "no!" of defiance to herdlike acceptability no matter how "settled" the particular opinion is claimed to be. Nor has truth ever been decided by a majority vote. All "modern" means is "recent" and everything that is recent inevitably becomes dated and old with time. Thus the so-called "modern" world of today is the old world of tomorrow. The supposedly enlightened opinions of today applauding the degradation, devaluing, and dispossession of our White people may well be considered foolish, backward, and insane tomorrow. The haters of White identity, White pride, and White advocacy are matched with their ignorance only by their arrogance in the thought that some kind of "Brave New World" has been reached that will never be questioned, never be critiqued, and never be discarded. Their recency in time does not give them potency of right. No so-called "end of history" has been reached as history has no end. The world of White emasculation has lasted a few decades but a few decades do not dictate to eternity. The "liberal" of tomorrow may not be the same as the so-called liberal of today and nor may this be the case with the so-called conservative either. These are mere words for a momentary period of time but they do not connote a vision. They are merely labels for a subservience to a status quo that may not be worth retaining. We have witnessed five decades of idiocy but that does not mean that the next five decades, centuries, or millennia must be the same.

It doesn't always have to be this way but we today live in a bizarre world in which it is considered more socially acceptable for a White man to triumphantly profess his homosexuality (and thus the unmentioned physical sexual perversion that that entails) than to even meekly profess an attachment to and loyalty to his White Race. In other words, it is considered more socially acceptable for a White man to profess sexual satisfaction through unnatural sex acts with other men than for a man to profess simple pride in and regard for his race which is certainly not *unnatural* regardless of whatever way it is looked at. The fact that no one is willing to openly discuss what homosexuals actually *do* with each other is proof enough though that there is a natural disgust for such things even if intellectually, people have been duped into thinking otherwise. On the other hand, there *is* a natural inclination in everyone to have racial *attachment* rather than disgust but this natural inclination has been intellectually *suppressed*. Thus the true haters, the haters of an extant, proud, assertive White Race, talk about their fight to "root out racism" but if racism were not deeply rooted and indeed as natural as the roots of any plant, it would not be considered necessary to "root it out," would it? Thus these people confess their hatred of the natural world. To be sure, they can suppress by numerous means, including persecutions, the natural racism in man—and indeed, the minds of our White people are locked in chains today—but they can never eliminate entirely the natural instinct of every creature on this earth to have allegiance to its own kind. Birds of a feather flock together and blood is thicker than water. It is racism which preserves the variety and *diversity* of life on this planet with which we are so inspired with awe. Without racism—regard for racial distinctions—there would soon cease to be different races of birds for example and nobody would waste his time and energy watching the mongrelized ugly bird flying about which would be the product of such a "raceless" mentality. By the same token, the same destruction of the beauty of man occurs when his mentality is raceless and when he views his natural racism as some kind of enemy. No one would think about chiding a canary for being unwilling to mate with a crow so why should we chide any White man for being unwilling to mate with a black? The example may seem inappropriate because men are not canaries or crows and yet the fact remains that we are all still part of Nature and her laws. Natural instinct teaches all species quite simply that exclusivity preserves and inclusivity destroys. Observe the distinctions and you will remain distinct; ignore the distinctions and your uniqueness will be obliterated. It is all so very simple but sometimes the most simple things pass people's notice for that very reason. Truth has never been complicated but unfortunately the more intelligent the being, the more it assumes it to be so. The White Loyalist is called upon to "defend" his views and yet no defense is necessary since his worldview is indeed in accordance with the world, i.e. Nature.

Observing and wishing to maintain the distinctions in man never had anything to do, by the way, with judging anybody by the color of his skin. Indeed, the railing against such judgments by King in the 60's, and generations since then, has been even more misplaced than the notion of "equality" that has also been of course idolized and bandied about. The reality is that making racial distinctions has, and had, nothing to do with personal judgments of anyone or of any kind. Indeed, individual personalities are totally irrelevant to the matter. Rather, what is at stake is being true to Nature's Laws whereby the natural diversity of the world is preserved. The man who disdains the integration of the races does not do so because he thinks that individuals of races different from his own are bad on some kind of personal basis. Rather, he simply wishes to preserve his own race with whom he naturally identifies and is loyal to. "Judging" individuals on the basis of race never enters the equation because the individual is not the issue. Whether we know non-white individuals of high character does not mean we should forsake White identity, White loyalty, or White advocacy any more than the fact that we all know women of high character means we should forsake our wives. Thus it must be realized that a phony argument has captivated the minds of our White people for decades, that we must either be raceless (i.e. "colorblind") or we must judge others by the color of their skin. This is a false dichotomy that never actually existed. I for one have never judged anybody by the color of his or her skin, least of all the billions whom I've never met, for this would indeed be asinine. However, that does not mean that I should not believe in an existence for White people, a consciousness for White people, a culture for White people, and a place in the sun for White people. These are not things that have anything to do with individuals of other races, their respective characters, and so forth and nor, for that matter, do they have anything to do with the individuals of my race. We have thus again been the victims of a canard: be raceless or judge others by the color of their skin when no such choice between the two options was ever necessary. There are good and bad characters in all races but that doesn't mean that our White people should be flushed down the drain by virtue of having a raceless mentality when it comes to our own White people, but full of race when it comes to helping the others. Loyalty to White people quite simply has nothing to do with judging others by the color of their skin and never did. Nor of course is any prejudice (pre-judging) involved, the word "prejudice" being yet another word falsely and routinely applied to the matter at hand.

Our sense of fair play has been manipulated against us by virtue of this atrocious canard that we must either be raceless (i.e. ignore our best interests as White people) or judge everyone by the color of his skin because, after all, it certainly does not seem fair to "judge" someone by virtue of something of which he or she had no control. That this has been a cruel hoodwinking of our White people is an understatement. What fair-minded White person would think it proper to judge this or that White man, black man, brown man, or yellow man as good or bad on the basis of color of skin thus overriding whatever good or bad qualities he or she individually possesses? It does not seem right because it isn't. We all know of White people with poor character which itself shows that a White skin does not necessarily signify a good character or that a non-white skin signifies a bad character. Thus it is immediately apparent that judgments as to the content of one's character on the basis of one's skin color are misplaced and nobody, upon reflection, would even disagree with that. In other words, if there are White people of poor character—and we thus *judge* these White people to be of poor character—the idea that we should not judge people by the color of their skin is an unobjectionable banality. That though has nothing to do with whether White people should be *preserved*. The matter is akin not to apples and oranges but rather to apples and giraffes. No White Loyalist has ever sincerely denied that there are good and bad characters in all races. It's just that this is not the point. We are not trying to preserve (and advocate) for White people because the individual character of black men is bad for we would do the same were every individual black man to be a saint. Rather, we are trying to preserve (and advocate) for White people because we feel that White people themselves have worth. One does not affect the other. One doesn't matter and the other does. This reality has been totally missed with the result that not one person in a thousand really understands what is at stake and what is at issue. It is like playing a game of baseball while thinking that the object is to *miss* the ball with the bat. We are told that we must not judge individuals by the color of their skin (of course!) as if that somehow means that we shouldn't care about the best interests of White people at all (of course *not!*). The minds of our White people are in chains. Witty propaganda slogans have taken our people down a false alley and this alley is leading us to a cliff. We are happily swinging our bats—content in our ignorance of the actual rules of the game—while our score on the scoreboard remains a big fat zero.

Notably, as the NAACP fights to advance *colored* people, and the National Council of La Raza fights to advance *hispanic* people, nobody ever accuses these organizations (and other non-white organizations), and their millions of members and sympathizers, of "judging" White people by the color of their skin and yet anytime any pro-*White* organization makes an appearance, it is immediately assumed to do just that. Thus the double-standard is plain, is it not? Simple logic dictates that if non-white organizations are spared all criticism for "judging" individual White people by the color if their skin, so should the White organizations for "judging" individual non-whites for theirs. Quite simply, discrimination in favor of one race has nothing to do with the "judging" of individuals of another race. Thus Martin Luther King's entire plea for a time when we would cease "judging" people by the color of their skin but rather by the content of their character was a plea that had nothing to do with the reality of the situation and thus not worth the idolizing since ascribed to it. If judging a person by the color of his skin is wrong as we all can agree, where is the supposed moral culpability of the White segregationist in the 1950's who did not engage in such judging? By the same token, the black separatist is not culpable either. Your preference for your own race has nothing to do with the personal character of the billions of individuals of other races and thus there is no reason for us, as White people, to feel any kind of guilt that White people past or present have engaged in an adverse judgment of that character. This of course extinguishes the entire guilty conscience that we have all been taught that we should have and that's why it is so important. We are not guilty! The policies and actions of our ancestors had nothing to do with judging any individual by the color of his skin. Never did we look at this black, brown, or yellow man and judge him bad because of his skin color and thus the entire prism into which we have looked concerning racial history has been a sad myth, sad because we have drawn the inference that since we shouldn't "judge" individuals on the basis of skin color, we shouldn't care about our own future as White people *at all*. A false charge has thus, in part, resulted in the abandonment and even disdain of everything we are and the sacrifice of our own best interests, indeed to the point where our own best interests are not recognized to even exist. To do so, after all, would be to "judge others by the color of their skin!" The most asinine myths are the most dangerous.

Whether we would will it to be different or not, no natural creature on earth ignores the difference between "us and not us." In fact, there is perhaps no thought or instinct more fundamental to life on this planet than this. All societal relationships are based upon it whether that of man, mouse, or mosquito. There are those who are part of "us" and there are those who are "not us." In Nature, this distinction is primarily decided by race and only secondarily by geography. Thus a lion, for example, is more likely to form a community with a fellow lion coming from a different geography than with a gazelle, tiger, or elephant who lives within his own geography. Genetics (race) trumps space. Furthermore, while a tiger may be a fellow cat, since he is not a fellow *lion*, the lion does not consider him one of "us" but rather, "not us." Thus the broad label of "cat" ascribed by men, like that of "bee," "bear," "ant" or that of any number of other beings, is not enough to erase the difference between "us" and "not us" as far as the various beings themselves are concerned. The creatures of this earth couldn't care less what labels men choose to ascribe to them; rather, they are only concerned, instinctively, with the exact genetic reality that confronts them: *whether this or that being is of the same race.* The members of one's community are strictly limited to individuals of the same race; black ants only live with black ants, red with red, grizzly bears with grizzly bears, bumble bees with bumble bees, and so with thousands of other examples. This does not mean that they "judge" the individuals of other races, only that they recognize a chasm between "us" and "not us." The generic words that we as *men* ascribe to animals do not bridge the chasm between them and thus, for example, the fact that we label grizzly, black, and polar bears by the same word "bears" does not mean that these various races can, should, or would form some kind of community together, for not only does genetics (race) (blood) trump space but it also trumps *language*, especially that of a race as far removed from them as is man. In other words, we can call the various similar types of omnivores "bears" all we want but that does not mean that there is, should be, or could be any such thing as a "bear" community irrespective of their various races. Nature couldn't care less what particular language men employ to describe the beings within it. What matters instead is the actual reality of the situation, the fact that the races of the beings in question are indeed different.

All of this seems pretty obvious in animals but why should it be any less the case with "man" which is likewise a generic term on par with "bear," "bee," "ant," and so forth? As with every race of animal there is the distinction between "us" and "not us," so too does this exist naturally among the races of *men*. Thus for us White people, "us" is our White people and "not us" are the other races, of both man and animal. "Man" is merely a generic label; it is merely a word used to describe beings that walk on two legs, can speak, and are capable of rational thought. The word does not denote a race but rather encompasses all races with such characteristics. Thus, likewise, there is no such thing as a "human race"; rather, there are races that we have adjudged to be human. Likewise, there is, strictly speaking, no such thing as "mankind" but rather there are "kinds (races) of men." There is no more natural community of "men" irrespective of race than there is a natural community of "bears," "bees," or "ants" irrespective of race. The labels that we ascribe, whatever they may be, do not alter the fundamental realities of Nature, try as we ignorantly might. I say "try as we ignorantly might" because let's face it, for hundreds of years people truly have been trying to change the natural reality of the world in an effort to make it conform to *language* rather than the other way around. How often have we heard people say that "there is only one race, the human race," for example, because of their own philosophical desire rather than obedience to the actual, real world around them? They want the world to fit the language rather than apply the language to the world as it is or, more importantly, have simply been caught up in the propaganda of our times without reflection. There is, again, no such thing as a "human race" but rather there are *races* of men or human *races* (distinctive races that walk on two legs, speak, and are capable of rational thought). That there are even those today who would deny that there are really races of men altogether, in favor of one supposedly monolithic "human race" of their own invention, just goes to show how deeply devoted they are to forcing the square block of Nature into the round hole of their philosophical desires. In reality, there are races of men just as there are races of bears, each in a state of Nature forming a community limited to its own respective race. Race in fact defines membership in the community. That the races of men have lately veered away from this natural disposition (lately in world history, certainly) is the problem, not that this natural disposition exists. Why indeed should we turn hysterically against our natural being in order to conform to an agenda, *any* agenda? If it were natural for the various races of men to live together and to form racially integrated "communities," forced busing, "fair housing" laws prohibiting racially restrictive covenants, and all other efforts to "desegregate" would never have been necessary. Racial integration is fundamentally unnatural; that is why people had to fight so hard to bring it about. "Community," as the name implies, relates to that which people hold in *common*, namely blood. Thus a "multi-racial community" is essentially a contradiction in terms. Notably, the word "community" bears no grammatical relationship to *geography*. This is well-illustrated by the fact that Jews, for example, are part of the same "Jewish community" regardless of where they happen to live, no matter how many thousands of miles they may be apart from one another, and even regardless of whether they happen to practice the Jewish *religion* or not. The word has to do with blood, ethnicity, and race, not a mere area on a map.

You will have noticed that I have not used the word "specie" in this discussion, referring instead to races of animals, races of insects, and, of course, races of men. This is because there is an inherent man-made value judgment bound up with the word "specie" that is not present with the word "race." A racial distinction exists in Nature whether we would want it to or not; it is a matter of *fact*, not a matter of (Man's) *classification*, unlike specie. Various races qualify as separate species only in the minds of men; in the minds of the various animals and insects themselves, all that matters is that they are different *races*. Thus distinctions between races and "species" have no value in Nature itself and serve to confuse men who have imputed value to them. Two members of different so-called "species," as commonly defined, are automatically members of different races; whether though two members of different races are also members of different species, as defined by men, is irrelevant to the discussion, for there aren't any more interracial communities in Nature than there are interspecial communities in Nature. *Race* is thus what characterizes Nature; whether racial distinctions "tax" the taxonomist enough to qualify also as special (in his eyes) is beside the point. As a mode of *classification*, the word "species" may have a certain use; as a method to exhibit *distinction*, it does not. Whether a grizzly bear and a black bear are *able* to interbreed (thus meeting the common definition of "species" as classified and manufactured by men) is pretty darn irrelevant as to whether they are in reality distinct beings (races) disposed to forming separate communities in Nature where such interbreeding wouldn't even take place, and whether such interbreeding would defy their natural instincts in fact.

I said earlier that all societies are based upon the distinction between "us" and "not us." This is the case even in the current non-racial American society; it's just that we have chosen geography, rather than race, upon which to base the distinction. Thus, in America, "us" is composed of Americans and "not us" is composed of non-Americans. Thus, unlike everywhere else in Nature, we have replaced the primary factor of race with that of the secondary factor of geography. Why, though, should we do this? We are *told* that we should, of course—and the vast majority of Americans do so without any thought at all—but where is the logic in being the only creatures on earth that place mere geography before race? We are told over and over again that "we are all Americans" but why should that matter so much more than the "we are all White" alternative as is so implicitly claimed and indeed demanded? We are expected to be "Americans first" but why should that matter more than being *White* first? It is considered proper to extol the colors of the American flag (or the colors of other flags should we live in other countries) but to extol the color *of our own skin* is today considered taboo. "To die for one's country" is considered by the present society the greatest honor but the idea of dying for one's *race* is never given any thought at all, let alone made the subject of positive social discourse. In sum, to be a patriot is to be lauded and to be societally blessed while to be a White advocate is to be criticized and societally condemned, and yet both concepts have their root in the "us" and "not us" distinction that governs all life and thus one would not expect them to be subjected to such disparate treatment. In other words, why should any man be reviled for placing his White Race first in his heart and mind while the "American" who puts America and Americans first in his heart and mind is applauded? Those who do the latter would be hard-pressed to justify the grossly disparate treatment between the two on any kind of rational or sensible grounds and yet so many of them condemn the *White* advocate without much of a thought at all. The so-called "Greatest Generation," for example, was supposedly so great because it defeated the Axis Powers in the Second World War in defense of America and Americans. Would though a generation of White people receive the same moniker today for defending *the White Race* in some equally titanic struggle? We know the sad answer to that. Why though should we have a country that we care about but a race that we don't? Why should we honor the defenders of the country but condemn the defenders of the race? Why should what is good for the goose be so strikingly bad for the gander?

Imagine a world where all of the fanfare that is currently devoted to our "us" as Americans were instead devoted to our "us" as White people. Would this be so wrong? And if so, why is the devotion to "us" as Americans so right instead? Why should geography trump our blood? We may "all be Americans" but our White Race existed thousands of years before there ever was such a moniker as "America" and hopefully it will continue to exist long after that name has passed into history as names of countries tend to do. States (polities) too have come and gone throughout history but the race remains. You love your country? This is understandable as it is only just to love the soil upon which you live, but do not forget though your own people in the process, that before your soil (geography) comes your blood (race), for how can we place more value in land than in our life itself? It may be argued that the placing of value in "us" as Americans does *not*, in fact, place land before life, but since those who are Americans are such because of their *geography*, it really does. In other words, without a *land* called America, there would be no Americans and no defense of American land and fellow Americans, of course. This is not the case with our White people whose existence is *not* based upon that of a particular land and indeed is independent of any land. The bond that exists between those whose "us" are Americans ends the moment one of them moves to and identifies himself with the nation-state across the border. When reflected upon, this is a pretty weak basis upon which to distinguish that which is "us" and that which is "not us" in this world; "us" can become "not us" pretty readily. On the other hand, by distinguishing "us" and "not us" on the grounds of *race*, no such back and forth parley is possible: you are "us" or "not us" based not on what you think or where you live but rather on what you *are*, which is unchangeable.

Again, the issue here is not whether we should love our country or not but rather whether we should really distinguish between our "us" and our "not us" on that basis. Why should we declare that we somehow have more in common with a black American than with a White Frenchman? Why should we have more concern for the well-being of yellow Americans over that of White Norwegians? Why should we care whether the White Serb is an "American" or not? Why should we care whether he resides outside a border on a map or maybe drives on the left side of the road? Why, too, should we be willing to fight and kill our fellow White people whenever a government—any government—tells us that we must? Why should we focus on the prosperity of the country rather than on our prosperity as a race? Why should we have a bond with everyone within our fifty United States that is superior to that of the bond with the White Canadian perhaps a mile away from us across a border, a border that only exists in our minds rather than is actually etched upon the earth at that? Borders are and always have been man-made. Our Race is not. Why should men be the only beings on earth to place borders before blood?

Bad ideas that we are raised with melt away when confronted with cold hard logic. The difficulty is in facilitating the confrontation. Bad ideas are like tires rolling down mountains, with tradition acting as a form of gravity, demanding that they have had the last word without any other word actually ever having had the opportunity to be spoken or heard. A new dawn is possible though if we can only realize that all thought is arbitrary, all values are transitory, unless they have a basis in the physical world and unless they do, their haloes are actually false crowns, hollow and brittle upon examination.

There is simply no sensible reason why the "American" in "White American" should matter more than the "White"; in "White American," in "White Spaniard," in "White South African," and in every other example. The fact that we are closer in *space* to those non-whites within our man-made borders or closer in *space* to those non-whites within the society in which we live does not mean that they have to, nor should, be our "us." So what if we live in the same country? So do ants, aphids, and armadillos. So what if we are all subjected to the same group of laws? So are those whom we personally hold in contempt. So what if we all speak English? We don't even all speak English anymore. So what if we all drive on the same roads? There are a lot of bad drivers on those roads too whom we wish were not there. So what if we all share the same values? We don't. So what if we all share the same history? We don't. So what if we all bleed red blood? So does a rhinoceros. We had no more say—unless we happen to be the traitors in governmental power—in choosing who lives in the same country and society as us than we did in choosing the color of our White skin, and yet our White skin, our White blood *is* us and thus a superior way of deciding who is "us" and "not us" than any mere *geographical* or *societal* accident. Just as for a normal man, his manhood is an inescapable part of his very identity and for a normal woman, her womanhood is an inescapable part of *her* identity, our race is an inescapable part of *our* identity. On the other hand, it is the *sick* man who denies his manhood, the *sick* woman who denies her womanhood, and the *sick* race that denies its racialhood. It is our being, our natural self, rather than an artificiality imposed from without. We are born with this identity before any thoughts or values are even imposed upon us. Every child is born with a consciousness of skin color as much as any other color but here the color signifies his very identity and tells him (and all others) who is "us" and who is "not us." Nature tells us who is "us" *by appearance alone* without a word ever having to be spoken or conjured. The race of each individual whom we encounter in this world is the trait we most immediately recognize and this signifies instinctively for us whom our "us" is. It is only society that tries to tell us that this is wrong in favor of a "we are all Americans" dogma designed to resign us to a "multiracial" society that we naturally would otherwise disdain.

Understand indeed that so much of the premise of the Americans are "us" dogma is that society, the country, and your very life is necessarily, inevitably, and irremediably "multiracial" and thus that you might as well forget about questioning it or resisting it. To do the latter would be "hateful," "bigoted," and even "un-American," or so it is claimed in some quarters even though the very founding documents of the United States of America were entirely written by White people for White people. The bottom line, as indicated before, is that we are expected to conform to a perverse, artificial society rather than make our society conform to us; to our natural, inherent identity and our best interests as a people and race. So many millions of our White people have sadly obliged, forfeiting their own will, their own interests, and sometimes indeed their own conscious desires. Conform! Be a herd animal! This is the message of the government, the media, the schools, and even the churches. Succumb to the thought that there is nothing for you to fight for when it comes to your own people and there's no way that you could get anywhere even if you did fight. Rather, just sink into your couch, turn on the boob tube, and swallow the mantra of White annihilation whole!

The truly free man though does not feel obliged to conform to any of society's demands; rather, he is determined to make society conform to his natural, unexpurgated self as a breed, as a blood, as a race. This is a freedom so much more important than the mere "freedom" of being able to say only what society claims is "acceptable" to say. The "freedom" to say only that which (the current) society demands is not much of a freedom and how could this be more true than in the case of White racial feeling, identity, and loyalty with which we are dealing? Thus for those who harbor such feeling, such identity, such loyalty, there are not many words more appealing than the word "non-conformist"! Yes, by the grace of ourselves, we do not conform with the idea that we should hate ourselves, that we should sacrifice our will to live as a people to misbegotten governments, societies, and newly-arrived habits and traditions; we say rather that "us" is what we *are* and not what it is "politically correct" to be. The truly free man does not care about being sensitive to the feelings of others as much as he cares about being *right*.

As part of the guilt complex that is foisted upon us, it is said sometimes that we should bear some kind of gratitude towards non-whites for their joining the American military and hurling themselves onto far-flung battlefields, supposedly at our behest, and supposedly somehow in the defense of our "freedom." This though, obviously, is not the kind of freedom that we have in mind and nor would we want these individuals to fight and die at our behest in the first place. In other words, the believer in White feeling, in White identity, in White loyalty did not send them, would not send them, and his freedom is not fought for by them. In reality, these nearly incessant wars have little to do with freedom for *anyone*, least of all for those who believe in a natural (hence separate) White identity, community, and country, but they are rather used as ploys by the government to drive home the idea that our "us" are Americans. "We're all in this together," and the like, such as "during a firefight I don't care what color the guy next to me is" and so forth. Obviously not, but the question is begged as to why soldiers must be perpetually placed into firefights by the government of the United States in the first place. The White loyalist did not place them there. No one disputes a man's courage based on his race; rather, the point is that a shared service in the military, or any other field for that matter, does not negate who our "us" truly is: our White Race, not "Americans" vs. "non-Americans" around the world as is claimed. Implicit in the idea that the White loyalist ("racist," as commonly referred to) should feel some kind of shame or guilt by virtue of non-white service in the military is that the "us" is Americans when this is simply not the case at all, just as many blacks have, past and present, realized that the *White* soldiers are not serving their "us" either (black people). All of this is very important to understand because there are few things worse than misplaced guilt and attacks upon our sense of honor. It is not the White Loyalist who seeks to use non-whites to literally fight his battles but rather the very politicians who are seeking to break down all White feeling, identity, and loyalty. In other words, it makes little sense to blame the White loyalist for the actions of those who are hostile to the very idea. *They* are the ones who throw non-whites into combat, not us.

To be sure, the 'Americans as us' idea is, at least in part, based on the supposition that Americans all share a special, mystical belief in freedom that binds them together in a way not shared by those who reside in the other lands of the world. This though is more rite than reality though it has been ingrained for so long that it is not given a second thought. In reality, *everybody* wants freedom but only to a certain extent, as total freedom is anarchy. (Most people, after all, would not care much for a "freedom" in which murder, rape, and robbery were legal and thus blessed by the State.) Thus there are certain freedoms—and not others—in *every* country and thus the notion that America has a special, unique, even exclusive claim to love of freedom that calls for all Americans to regard themselves as "us," and the rest of the world as "not us," is flawed. Furthermore, consider the fact that the very claimed foreign policy of the federal government is to promote freedom around the world *because allegedly everyone wants it*. If everyone wants it, we cannot be unique in that regard and if everyone wants it but many are denied it by their governments, is it really just to deem all Americans as "us" on the basis of a shared belief in freedom while rejecting the rest of the world as "us" even though they also share that belief? Again, the idea breaks down. If a belief in freedom determined who is "us" and who is "not us," we could not very well divide the world into Americans and non-Americans since many, if not all, non-Americans also believe in it. So, we are back to mere geography once again notwithstanding the claim that our "values" set us so far apart from everybody else. Everywhere men would like to speak their minds, practice their religion, and not be assaulted in their homes and on the streets. This is not an exceptional wish anywhere.

The call for you then is to understand that your "us" is what you *are* and not where you were born, what political or geographical label may be ascribed to you, or what particular thoughts happen to go through your head. Your "us" is not dispelled or dissipated by your nationality, your religion, your politics, your economic class, or the clothes you wear for that matter. You can speak English, German, Russian, or even Chinese or Swahili without your "us" changing in the least. You can reside at the North Pole or in the tropics, like a big government or a small one, prefer George Washington or prefer the Czar, call yourself a conservative, liberal, libertarian, fascist, communist, or whatever and yet your "us" remains the same: White people. Your skin is your uniform before any tunic imposed by a government. Your race is your being whether United States of America remain in existence, whether there is a border on a map between Frenchmen and Germans, whether the Flemish and Walloons continue to live together in a polity called Belgium, whether Quebec remains part of Canada, or whether a million other man-made distinctions continue to exist. Your distinction, with precedence over all others, is what *Nature* made, not man. You hence rejoin the rest of the beings in the world. Your justification is your *existence* and you need not have more. The thoughts that have afflicted us are like the leaves that come and go with the season while the tree, your race, remains. Your physicality trumps the mentality of geography. Your appearance negates the need for a question. Your "us" is your being that needs no words wherever you are. The truest identity is that which is discerned on sight: your race.

Nature herself points the way but because Man has divorced himself from the natural world, he fails to see it. Losing the guide of Nature, his mind becomes his own worst enemy, for being capable of abstract thought, abstractions come to dominate him, to wage war against his very being; his mental power gives him the ability to muster an endless amount and variety of thoughts regardless of whether they are conducive to his natural, and hence racial, survival or not. Thus Man has burdened himself with concerns about lines on maps, religions, economic classes, and the like when all along his true being, his true distinction, his true significance, his true "us" stared back at him when he simply gazed upon his reflection in a mirror: his race, his blood, his kind. It has never been anything *other* than that. *Today's* world is the perversion, not the eons of the past where our "us" was at least more recognized than it is today, though still flawed and imperfectly, for all around us is race in its unashamed and undiluted splendor. Every bird exhibits race, every bee exhibits race, every bear exhibits race, every creature everywhere exhibits race, and yet we've been told that thoughts of race are wrong! How though can thoughts of race be wrong when the whole natural world is guided by them? What makes a lion a lion but his race? What makes a sparrow a sparrow but his race? What makes a red fox a red fox but his race and what separates him from a gray fox but his race? "Foxes" they may both be but their difference is their being! Do we really wish to destroy that being...in foxes or in men? Should we really allow artificiality to trump naturality?

Let us though consider the matter in perhaps simpler, more "human" terms: who in this world should we *side* with? Shouldn't we in fact side with our own people? (We can't side with everyone for sides *do* exist.) Even the geographical "us" with which we are currently burdened ("Americans," for example, versus "non-

Americans") acknowledges that various people and States around the world have their own *interests*. What then are ours as White people? Shouldn't they, at a minimum, include our continuing to *exist*, to retain a culture of our own, to have a space that we can call our own, to preserve further our very lives? How many of us today are concerned about the present and future of elephants, of whales, of polar bears, of eagles, and many other creatures; do not our White people have *at least* as much value as they do in our own eyes and thus should we not also be supported and pre-served? Thus if it is praiseworthy to avowedly seek to preserve the existence of polar bears, how can anyone say with a straight face that it is not praiseworthy to avowedly seek to preserve the existence of our own White people? Or are we so sick today as a people that we would rank the racial existence of polar bears highly but consciously disparage and devalue that of our own kind? Are we so full of self-hate that we would proudly protect the races of *animals* around the world but gleefully and "proudly" forsake the protection of our own? Aesthetically speaking, polar bears are delightful creatures but did they give us Shakespeare, Da Vinci, Edison, Beethoven, ad infinitum? Can we thank polar bears for electricity, running water, sewing machines, airplanes, et cetera? How many millions of people are concerned about the future of polar bears and other creatures; would that these same millions and more be concerned about the future of White people too! Everyone has an understanding of the need of every race of animal to have its own habitat; have we forgotten our own need in that regard? If it is praiseworthy to seek the preservation of animal races, should it not also be praiseworthy to seek the preservation of the race of White people, the preservation of its genes, its genotype, upon this earth? As a society, we are taking steps, and have been taking steps, to preserve the existence, the genotype, of numerous creatures. Where though is the effort, as a society, to preserve the existence, the genotype, of our own White Race? If the one is praiseworthy, should not the other be as well?

Conversely, who ever heard of someone being *denounced* for

caring about the preservation of animal races? Who ever heard of someone being smeared as a "racist" (intended as a disparagement, that is) for wanting to protect the races of whales, for example, from whaling? Who ever heard of elephant lovers being denounced as "racists" for wanting to stop poachers from killing them for their tusks? And yet the point is indeed the preservation of their *race*! Can we in turn say that the *White* race of men is being preserved when we don't even have a habitat of our own, when our culture has become nigrified, and when our race is mongrelized with the other races at will? We say that we love the beauty of Nature's creatures; would that we would love that of our own kind too! If we are willing to love creatures who are clearly "not us," shouldn't we also be willing to love "us"? Why on earth should we be more reluctant to say openly that we wish to preserve the White Race than we are to say that we wish to preserve the humpback whale, or the condor, or the spotted owl, or innumerable other examples? Indeed, the minds of our White people have been in chains to the point where a situation exists where we are willing, eager, and proud to fight to preserve the races of various animals but unwilling, reluctant, and ashamed to fight to preserve that of our own. Let someone try to offer a sensible reason why we should support the races of animals but not support that of our own race, why we should invest so much time, money, and effort to support the races of animals but invest so little to support our own race, why the races of animals matter but the race of White people doesn't. He will be hard-pressed. The only explanation is the lack of love that we currently have for ourselves as unique, distinct, and worthwhile beings on this earth. We frown at our own existence; I would yearn that we smile! For make no mistake: there can be no long term preservation of a race, of our race, unless it is *racial*, that it recognize and appreciate race in all things. For only with a racial consciousness can there be a racial culture, and only with a racial culture can there, in today's world, be racial exclusivity, and only with racial exclusivity can there be racial preservation.

There is a great chasm between praise and condemnation

that behooves us to be consistent, that if we praise something on one basis, we should not very well condemn an analogous situation that operates on the same basis. Thus I turn to another example, in this effort to break the chains of our mental slavery, that is perhaps closer to home for our White people today in light of our present detachment from Nature: sports.

If it is praiseworthy to root for one's own *high school sports team*, it is hard to fathom why it should not also be praiseworthy to root for one's own *race*, and do we not also root for our own team whether its play be fair or foul? It's *our* team! That's what matters. We always look at every play from our team's perspective and we leave the other team's perspective to *its* fans. It is not our task to sing the praises of the other team but rather to sing the praises of our own. That this is so natural and expected is indicated by the fact that nobody ever gives the matter a second thought. We root for our own team and that's that. We have pep rallies for our team, marches for our team, and wear our team's regalia with pride. To not have much enthusiasm for one's team is to evince a lack of school *spirit* and this is bad. In any event, while some may be lacking in *enthusiasm* for the doings or exploits of one's own team, nobody ever roots for the *visiting* team; indeed, who ever heard of high school students *against* their own team? A pep rally during school in which the loyalties are divided between the home team and the soon-to-be-arriving visiting team? Band members refusing to play the school song or even breaking out into the song of the visiting team? Students shunning the colors of their team in favor of the colors of the visiting team?

How silly would it be if the support of students for their own team were to be decried as "prejudice," "hate," "bigotry," and the like? Can you imagine how incredulous a student would be were you to berate him for rooting for his team? He would likely look at you as if you were an escaped lunatic.

That we take our sports teams very seriously is a truism with which no one can find objection. Many billions of dollars a year are spent rooting for them at all levels, there are entire television networks devoted to covering them, players are "drafted" as if into the military, their exploits are discussed as seriously as politics, and their victories and defeats assume the character of triumphs and agonies in the hearts of millions if not billions of people. What though is really at issue but a mere *game*, a fantasy, an abstraction? Its value is totally self-contained; the value of sports is only within sports itself and only has the value which we ourselves attach to it. And yet it is important to men and women everywhere and no one bothers to justify that importance. What begins in high school and even earlier continues through our lives and is promoted, embraced, and applauded by society.

Well, *isn't our White Race our team too* but a team whose stakes are far higher than that of any mere sports game? We too have a struggle to win in this world but it is a struggle for existence and livelihood rather than for mere points on a scoreboard. If enthusiasm for mere sports is so high, enthusiasm for our concrete *race* should be much higher by virtue of plain logic. Do we not have more to lose as a race if we neglect its best interests than we have to lose if our particular sports team loses on the field? Should we not be more serious about that which is in fact serious than that which is merely fun?

If it is right to have "school spirit," must it not also be right to have "White spirit"? If it is right to rally support for our particular sports team, must it not also be right to rally for our White racial team? If we are proud of our sports team, can we not also be proud of our racial team? Our skin is our uniform and the field we must win is the earth. There is no shedding this skin and thus no possible trading of it for another color unlike the situation with every other kind of uniform. Our instinctive and rightful allegiance to it is established at birth and since we wear it so long as we live, our rightful allegiance to it lasts that lifetime. Just like every other uniform, our skin color should tell all, instantly, where our loyalties lie.

I would challenge anyone to explain why it is that rooting for a particular sports team makes more sense than rooting for our White Race, why we should devote billions of dollars to the promotion of sports teams but should devote little to nothing to the promotion of our White Race, why we should defend the reputation of our sports team but refrain from defending the reputation of our White Race, and why we should be loyal to our sports team but be disloyal to our White Race. Again, is it not so that our White Race is also a team, in a different form, true, but a team nonetheless?

It makes no difference that we were born into our White racial team instead of being able to choose it. It is our team regardless. Why should the matter of choice matter at all? We didn't choose our parents either but we still have love for and loyalty to them. Is it not true that even children put up for adoption, and who thus haven't seen their parents since birth, still retain this love and loyalty towards them, towards people they never even met? Furthermore, often times we do not consciously choose to be parents ourselves and yet we still have an instinctive love for and loyalty to our own children. We didn't choose our own siblings either but we still have love and loyalty to them too. There is a natural love towards our family; it is a bond not of conscious thought, not determined by reasoning or thinking the matter through at all but rather is a matter of *blood*. Our parents, our children, and our siblings may do things we disdain, and we may wish that we could have chosen different ones, but they *are still our blood*.

This is true of our race as well. As with our immediate family, so with our racial family. We know that many of our White people have done things that we disdain and that there is no shortage of bad characters in our history, and yet the fact remains that our White people are still our people. Every White man, woman, and child is related to us, is our blood or, as one might more readily put it today, is of the same genetic strain. Our race is our "us," our family, our team. Our White Race is ours and we are its. Again, we belong to this race regardless of the polities in which we live or the language that we speak. Indeed, this race existed before there *were* any polities and before there *were* any languages and will, if we break the chains of our mental slavery at least, exist long after such polities and languages have either ceased existing themselves or have changed massively. Long before there were ever United States of America, a United Kingdom, or a European Union, or before there were ever English, Greek, Czech, or other languages, there were White people, and while polities and languages come and go throughout history, the race that forged those polities and languages remains. Blood matters more than any particular form of government, lines on a map, or the form of speech that we employ. Our race transcends all of these things. It is our team wherever it goes and indeed, since all of us are of the same genetic strain, a strain that distinguishes us from all the other races, *it is our family as well.* The blacks are right to call each other "brother" or "sister" because they indeed possess their own racial family and so do we as White people! Ironically then, what White people tend to consider a source of amusement, mystery, or even disdain—that blacks often refer to each other as brother or sister—is instead something that is worthy of respect and appreciation and something that should likewise be customary with our *own* race. They have their racial family and we have ours. Our racial family may not be as close as our immediate family but it is still our family. One cannot truly justify the love for one without justifying love for the other. You have brothers and sisters of your immediate family, you have kin of your extended family, and you have brothers and sisters of your racial family; all tied by blood, not by thought processes. All created by Nature rather than fabricated by man.

That there are those who would vehemently deny all of this simply shows how far we have sunk, and how confused we have become, as a people. They perceive man as a mere atom, an atom among other atoms but totally independent of them without any responsibility to anyone or anything but himself, that he has no roots and no destiny, no ancestors and need be concerned about no descendants, and that there is no guide for him in life at all other than what he comes up with in his own head. And they wonder why there is so much crime, so much depression, so much drug use, and all in all so much lack of self-respect, self-confidence, self-discipline, and self-esteem in the people! The way they would have it, all rests on the individual, but the reality is that man in his loneliness needs more than himself. We *want* roots, we *want* a destiny, and we *want* to believe that the world does not begin and end with our own individual selves. Otherwise, is it not a fact that we are all losers in the end, no matter how many pleasures we may have enjoyed during our brief individual life on earth? For in the end, the individual inevitably loses.

With racial feeling, with racial consciousness, with racial love, with racial loyalty though, we have something far greater than our individual selves which can and will, if we allow it to, give us a purpose and meaning to our lives which may not otherwise exist. When we look upon the world as a team, as a racial family, we know what we must do: strive to advance it, to benefit it, to look out for it, to be proud of it, to root for it. How little this truly has to do with "hatred," "prejudice," or "bigotry" as our White people have been so thoroughly propagandized! At most, it means that you are *willing* to hate but upon reflection, that goes for *anything* a person loves. If, for example, you have a son and you love him of course, you will be *willing* to hate the pederast who lurks outside his school. If you have a wife and love her of course, you will be *willing* to hate he who would contemplate raping her. If you have love for your country, you will be *willing* to hate the army contemplating the invasion of it. In other words, under these scenarios, hate is simply a mechanism to employ in the defense of that which you love, as necessary.   It is a tool of defense, not some kind of mystical force of malevolence as is so commonly made out, especially in the propaganda attacks against our White people. It can be an entirely justifiable and indeed desirable emotion. By hating threats to that which you love, you tend to preserve that which you love. If some scoundrel is slashing at your children with a butcher knife, love is not the emotion you need at the forefront of your mind at that moment in order to save their lives but rather hatred, a righteous hatred for he who would harm that which you love.

How telling it is indeed that in our sick society, where any indication of Whiteness is considered foul, that the label of "haters" is reserved almost entirely by the media and government for those who love White people and want a future for them. Nobody ever calls the misnamed "civil rights movement" a "bunch of haters" while pro-White groups are called that without hesitation and yet, is it not a fact that the so-called civil rights movement *hated* conditions in society as they were and hence resolved to change them? Whether you hate people, policies, conditions, ideas, or whatever are distinctions without a difference as the emotions, or sentiment, is the same. Why should pro-White groups be the only groups in society that are called "hate groups" as a matter of course?

Nobody ever calls the American revolutionaries "haters" and yet they hated King George III and the lack of American representation in the British parliament. Would there be United States of America if they hadn't?

Nobody ever calls Christian missionaries "haters" and yet is it not a fact that Christianity seeks to displace, even eliminate the native religions of those it seeks to convert? And could not adherents of these native religions fairly interpret such an effort to be "hateful"?

Nobody ever calls environmentalists "haters" even though they clearly hate the destruction of the environment. Nobody ever calls professed "animal rights" activists "haters" even though they clearly hate to see people wearing fur. Nobody ever calls capitalists "haters" even though most of them would probably admit hating communism. Nobody ever called Americans "haters" during the two world wars of the 20th century even though they were clearly involved in the killing of their claimed enemies in Europe and Asia. Has anyone ever called the Founding Fathers (revolutionaries), the Catholic church (Christians), the Sierra Club (environmentalists), PETA (animal rights), the Club for Growth (capitalists), or the U.S. Army "hate groups"? Surely nobody thinks that the U.S. Army, for example, conquered Western Europe in World War Two through acts of "love"?

Even true black separatists, who hate the mingling of the races as much as the White, are generally, if not always, spared the label or accusation of being "haters."

No, it is only the White man who holds the preservation of his race and culture dear to his heart who is routinely considered afflicted as a "hater" while innumerable movements and individuals throughout history and today are left unassailed in their own hatred. The great irony is that not only does the White Loyalist in actuality hate *less* than these movements and individuals past and present but that as soon as a White man, woman, or child offers any kind of opinion even mildly sympathetic to the preservation of the White Race, *he or she* finds himself or herself on the receiving end of hatred. So, pardon me if I refuse to accept the nonsense that we White Loyalists are deserving of any kind of singling out as "haters" or participants in "hate groups" when no other cause, groups, or individual anywhere is labeled in such a manner. Why should those who seek to preserve their race and culture be deemed "haters" anyway? The minds of our White people are in chains for thinking so. Again, while innumerable other causes and individuals hate to their hearts' content without censure, our present society is so sick that it condemns only the White man as a "hater" who is merely loyal to his race. Everything under the sky can be done to dispossess us of what is ours—including the flooding of our country with non-white immigrants, the firing of White workers so as to make way for non-white workers, the peddling of a non-white trash culture of sex obsession to our children, and even the legalization and now overt promotion of interracial marriage (mongrelization)—and yet we are conditioned to believe that any opposition to such assaults upon our prosperity and continued survival as a race would be "hateful" (and hence to be disdained lest we be labeled as "haters"), and yet the assaults themselves are presumably to be considered some form of "love"? One could weep for the insanity of man. We have been befuddled for so long and so thoroughly that grass is blue and the sky is green in our eyes. And our heroes have become villains and our villains have become heroes. Those who break the chains of their own mental slavery can expect to be called villains, haters, and worse but such is the price of true freedom.

The whole "hate" smear business is so worth mentioning—and at several different junctures at that—because it is so endemic. It is a psychological weapon wielded against any budding of a proud, assertive, considerate, conscious White Race. It is intended as a bludgeon with no contact even being needed to be made. It has been enormously successful. Men who know that our people have been wronged or at least perceive of the hideous double-standard have, by the thousands or even by the millions, kept their mouths shut for fear of the "hate" smear. Thus the mental slavery of our people as a whole extends to the physical slavery of those whose minds are *not* so much in chains. We do not live in a time of courage; rather, we live in a time of "sensitivity" and this towards every group but our own. We live in a time of a supposed "democratic" will but our White people today have no will. We live in a time of "love" but our White people today have been turned away from loving themselves. I drive the point home because the point must be driven home. We would never deny any other people their love of self so why should love of self be denied to us? We are not bound by a decadent present nor a decadent or inferior past but rather can form our own will.

There is indeed a White people on this earth. There is indeed a White Race and no, the word "race" is not a bad word. It is the word that reflects the fundamental reality of all life and it is particularly appropriate since we are indeed in a "race," a competition, with the other races, the other teams, on this earth. If we do not side with ourselves, we lose. We must discriminate in favor of our race, our team, or it loses. We have our own unique personalities but we are still part of the race, the team, our "us." The only civil "rights" that should matter to us are that of our own: our power, our strength, our will. The only right that should matter to us is our own. If we end up dominating the field, that is as it should be. Who ever heard of a team shaving its own points or donating some to its rivals?

We should disdain the racial diversity of society because we desire the diversity of men, wishing to preserve their distinctions, their uniqueness, their natural selves. We should disdain the idea of equality (sameness) of man because men are not in fact the same as one another and nor are the races which are composed of men. Rather than equality, let there be distinction. Rather than forbearance, let there be assertion: of ourselves.

We as White people do exist for our eyes do not lie. We are not individuals who just happen to be White but rather are White people who are also individuals, individuals of a race. We each play our particular position on the team but that hardly means that the team, the race, does not exist. This man here is an auto mechanic, that man there is a computer programmer, another is a fireman, and still another a welder; they work for a personal living but there is also a racial living to their work, fulfilling the needs of the team, the race. The individual comes and goes but the race remains; at least it should, and *will*, without our minds being in chains. The coming and going of the individual player does not mean the end of the team, does it?

It matters not why we are White any more than it matters why our parents are our parents, our siblings are our siblings, or our children are our children. As we should be loyal to our families, we should be loyal to our race. The loyalty naturally exists simply because...they are *ours*. From the seed of our ancestors we spring and from us shall our descendants spring. Kind after kind, like after like, blood after blood, the bond of Nature precedes and succeeds all diversions that tickle the fancy of the moment in the minds of men.

"Civil rights" were "rights" in the minds of black people in the 1950s and 1960s simply because they wanted them. *Their desire became their right.* So should it be for us, for the best interests of *our* people, no other interests likewise to be considered any more than the best interests of Whites were considered by the black "equality" seekers. We though should refuse to use "equality" as a means because we are *better* than that. No such demagoguery suits the taste of the upright man and who ever heard of a team merely wanting to be "equal" to the others? And what sports fan ever likes a *tie* game?

We as White people have swallowed so much silliness, so many propaganda gimmicks, so much subterfuge, so much delusion. Can we yet extricate our minds from these chains that ensnare us? Can we yet come to understand that we owe no people but ourselves, that the only possible sin that we can commit as a people is to ignore our own interests as that (White) people, and that the current society with its demands of White guilt, forbearance, and denial is hostile to those best interests? Can we not come to understand that racial integration is a profoundly *destructive* activity to White culture, White genes, and White lives? That White culture, White genes, and White lives and yes, White *freedom* should have at least as much value to *White people* as the achievement of so-called "equality" did to black people, as open borders does to brown people, as "living the American dream" does to yellow people, and on and on? That we as White people have the prerogative to have a place in the sun, to chart our own destiny, and to exert our own will as much as anybody else? That there is more "hate" in White guilt, forbearance, and denial than there is in White assertion, loyalty, and pride? That the genetic survival of no bear, fish, owl, or any other animal race can possibly be more important to us than the genetic survival of our own *White* race? That racial love and loyalty need no more justification than family love and loyalty? That all lines on maps are artificialities and thus of less importance than the race, our race, which is *real*?

Can we remove our minds from the media, government, and school propaganda manipulation that lock, keep, and tighten our minds in chains? Can we dare to think outside of them; can we recognize them for what they are, melt them with our will, break them with our spirit, and overthrow them with our love?

Chapter Two
Exhortation

A White people whose minds are no longer in chains, a proud White people conscious of itself and assertive of its own best interests in all things and at all times, a White people that has divested itself of the fallacy of guilt that has been heaped upon it by a controlled, manipulative media, the victory of allegiance towards race over that of space, this I espouse. Would you join me in so doing?

For the youth, this is the dynamism that they have been searching for. For the old, this is the morality to which they, when they were young themselves, were favorably inclined. For those neither old nor young, the handwriting is simply on the wall, exposed beyond question: the grotesque double-standard from which our people suffer and by which we have suffered long, too long, without complaint. Time it is to resist! It is time to quit swallowing the claimed castor oil (in reality poison) that has been meted out to us, to quit allowing ourselves to be docile sheep allowing our culture, our genes, and our very lives to be shorn from us at will. And if we have indeed broken the chains that had ensnared our minds and hence our actions as well, do we not also wish now to hurl those chains away from us as far as possible? For we look with contempt upon them, as well as upon ourselves, for letting them bind us for so long. Hence we say, away with you and don't come back! We have had enough of your binds; we have had enough of your stifling of our true freedom. Your presence is a source of shame to us; your clanging still echoes in our ears. Would that you had never existed! But alas we cannot change the past...but the present and future is within our realm and mighty ones can they be! The vestige of our slavery can become but a phantom...should we deign to remember it at all!

Of course I presume that you have come with me with your thoughts. Dare I presume so much? Surely you recognize that which has been denied to us; would that you would be ready to affirm instead! Do not tell me that you are still mired in the muck of "equality." Do not tell me that you believe that, even if "equality" were to be true, your White people are indeed treated equally under the present order? Let me challenge you then: are the best interests of White people *as White people* given equal (the same) consideration as those of black people under the present order? Is there "affirmative action" for White people? Are there television stations devoted to White people as White people? Are there scholarships earmarked for White people as White people? Is there a "White History Month"? Do the politicians care about "the White vote" as much as they prostrate themselves over the black and brown? Where are our White colleges? Where are our "civil rights"? Where is the prosecution for "hate crimes" for the numerous crimes committed against us because of hatred for *our* race? Where is our "Congressional White Caucus"? I could go on and on but is there really any need? You know the story because you have lived it, have witnessed it, and have been confronted with it. You know the story because you are not dumb, deaf, or blind. Your mind may have been in chains but that has never affected your senses! Your senses have never lied to you; you have simply ignored them. You have been told to be colorblind but when has any kind of blindness ever been good? You have eyes to see but need an unfettered mind to *discern*. Do you discern now, I hope?

Fine. Let them have it their way. They have written us out of their notion of "equality," their notion of "civil rights," and their notion of "tolerance." So be it, my Brothers and Sisters, for such demagoguery ill suits us and after all, two wrongs don't make a right! No, rather than "equality," let us say *quality*; rather than "civil rights," let us say *power*; and rather than "tolerance," let us say *deserving*! Let the distinctions, the qualities of this world rule the day; let the power of our White race not be abridged or sacrificed in any way; and let us choose what should be deserving to be part of *our* society! *That* is the only e-quality that we can embrace, the only "civil rights" that we can demand, the only "tolerance" that we can stomach: quality, power, and that which is deserving! For White people!

The clinking remnant of our former chains of mental slavery grows fainter in our ears...but can we make it fainter still? Can we yearn for greatness rather than mediocrity, the exceptional rather than the "popular," the yearning rather than the resigned? And when, in the present day, do we ever hear of the word *glory* even being uttered, let alone sought? Can we make that word, that blessed word, heard again and felt, one day?

Do not speak to us about "freedom" unless it include duty, or duty unless it include honor, or honor unless it include glory! Where is the glory today, the honor today in our forbearance as a people, our self-denial, our prostration? Or have we forgotten that men do not live by bread alone? When has a great people ever taken the path of *least* resistance? Have we, in our present weakness, forgotten that resistance builds *strength*?

But alas, my Brother and Sisters, strength is not valued today! We would rather be accommodating than strong, yielding than firm, "sensitive" than right...until you have joined me with your thoughts that is! For now we break the binds! This is the great hope, my great hope.

"Equality" is and always has been the cry of the inferior, the effort to lower that which is higher through the assertion of a supposed "equality" of everybody. But to destroy the chasm between men, and *the races of men*, is to destroy that which makes Man man! May we perish the thought from our hearts, vacate it from our minds! For all men are *not* equal, nor are they created equal, and nor will they become equal! Thus speaks *our* love of man. Nature is on our side, the world is on our side, if we have the will to affirm it as it is. May the subterfuge melt before our fiery sun of truth! May the fantasies expire with a final shudder! May the real world be loved again!

Not the equality of men do we espouse but rather the equality of *mem*bership in our White Racial Family; not the non-existent sameness of men but that we White people are all part of the same race, blood, breed, kind! That is the equality that we embrace, the only equality concerning men that has any truth to it.

This is an equality that is true to life: "we (White people) are all White people." The equality of self-evidence, the equality of our senses, the equality of "us," the equality of all being part of the same team. Though unequal to one another (not the same as), the catcher and the pitcher and the left fielder, for example, are all part of the same team! This is the equality of mutual loyalty, the equality of mutual allegiance, the equality of our mutual *identity*! Hail the equality of identity! Not the equality of that which is within two lines on a map but rather the equality of all of us being part of the same racial family! That is our identity, our equal attachment to it! *There* is an equality that we can love, together!

But alas, the old habits die hard...do you still find yourself their supplicant? Are your backs still bent even now under their weight? Does the false dogma of equality of *men* still contort and confound your tongues? Have the will to stand up straight, to shrug your shoulders, and seal your mouths, if need be, until your tongues obey your will! Have the will to assert a new yes, envision a new horizon, conceive of a new dawn! For old habits die hard but they do die, nonetheless! And the youth have not had the time to become so habitual! Thus I tailor this exhortation to the mindset of the young. Let them lead the way for the chains upon their minds have not been so fixed, not so locked, as otherwise. They know that the present painting need not be painted with the same strokes of the brush forever and ever, that we can paint differently as we choose. The world is their oyster, after all, not their straitjacket! The concrete has been poured but has not yet hardened with them—or with me either if I can dare to say that I am still young! Young, middle, or old though are all still capable of the revolutionary spirit and can break their own chains of mental slavery. For no brain need be in a box forever! And even the heaviest chains corrode under the assault of the elements, the truths of the natural world! Glory be to those truths which are in fact *your* truths. Glory be to the restoration of the natural man with race permeating to his very soul! For that is indeed *the* truth of the natural world, that every race is racist!

Let us though delve into more meat of the matter: the struggle for the victory of race over space, the victory of racial identity, loyalty, and attachment over the phony, meaningless patriotism of our age, and certainly that victory over the worship of raceless and spaceless *cash*, for that matter! How glad we are that loyalties are like forks in roads: very clear to the choice once they are at least fathomed. There is a great sense of satisfaction to have such clear choices before us, once we are made conscious that there are indeed choices! To have a choice is to have a power but the choice must first be recognized to exist before that sense of power can be felt! We have the choice to put our stock in race, in space, or maybe some other collective but matters of individual selfishness we can reject out of hand for our purposes because there is no "we" to them by their nature. In other words, we are talking about what is our we, our "us," not whether we as individuals desire this or that for our individual selves. Materialism has to do with the individual and thus cannot be the determinant of our *us*! Materialism is a personal covet but has nothing to do with our *identity*; identity is what we are talking about, not the place that material, financial things play in our individual lives. Thus rather than some kind of a collective struggle for personal greed—a struggle that cannot exist because personal greed is always *personal* and at someone else's expense—the struggle is for *us*. The problem is that we have, for so long, had the wrong "us" in mind! We failed to realize that our race is our "us"!

What the "individualists" and the "libertarians" forget is that there is *always* a collective, one way or the other! There is always an "us" and a "not us" in this world, the only question being the criterion by which they are determined, and "us" and "not us" are indeed collectives by definition! The minute the individualist and the libertarian use the word "us," they are invoking a collective. The moment that individuals band together into any kind of group, they are creating a collective. The moment that the word "Americans" is spoken, a collective is spoken...there is no use escaping it! The individual can assert his individuality all he wants but there is still a collective of some kind dear to his heart. The libertarian can talk about how much he believes in freedom of thought and action all he wants but he still invokes his countrymen! "Us and not us" are the nature of the world. No one fights for freedom alone. No one is without ties. This is a fundamental truth of the world. Would that we would acknowledge it with eyes wide open and clean ears! Individuals are always individuals *of* something. Libertarians always desire liberty for *people*. It is never just the individual! The name of a city is that because *we* name it so. *We* are bound by the rules of the road. The original, true meaning of the word "nation" is a people, a tribe, a *we*. Taxes are a collective, police departments are a collective, hospitals are a collective, and society itself is a collective. Have we forgotten that there is no *society* without the *social* and that the *social* requires more than the *individual*?

But you ask, my Brothers and Sisters, why is today's patriotism "phony"? It is phony because it is hollow. It is phony because it is raceless. It is the idea that there is some kind of bond between people just because they find themselves between two lines on a map! It is the idea that space trumps race! We wonder how such a silliness could have been maintained for so long. An illegal immigrant, brown Mexican invader crawls across the border, evades detection, is granted amnesty by some traitor congressmen, and is now bestowed the status of being part of "us"? Are you kidding? And we are expected to link arms with him "should our nation (i.e. traitor government) call" us to go off to fight peoples thousands of miles away who had never heard of us nor we of them, as well as members of our own racial family? We are supposed to have a greater bond with those of every hue under the sun than those of our own hue? What kind of patriotism ("love of fatherland") is that? How can there be true patriotism, love of *father*land, without the recognition that we are *Brothers and Sisters,* and how can we be Brothers and Sisters without being related by blood, i.e. race? Hence the meaning of true patriotism: Brothers and Sisters of a racial family defending and fighting for their fatherland! On the other hand, the "patriotism" of mere lines on a map, of every person within it merely on the basis of their being able to walk, talk, and engage in some rational thought, the patriotism of "we all pay taxes to the same government," that indeed is phony! But you say, "what about the patriotism of freedom-loving citizens of all races?" Well, isn't it true that people all over the world love freedom to varying extents; what then would become of our "patriotism" were we to include them too? There could be no more fatherland but rather we would have a borderless globalism! Our land could not come first before other lands because our supposed "patriotism" would include them all! What, then, would be the point of "patriotism"?

Multi-racial patriotism is a monster for it forces, or at least demands, that we place fellow "Americans" (or other geographically-based people) first in our hearts and minds and actions regardless of their race over those of our own race in other countries, that we disdain, disclaim, and disfavor the bond of blood in favor of lines upon a map. Resist this, my Brothers and Sisters! Resist such an artificiality, such a *plastic* way of looking at the world! Know that there is no multi-racial "people"; rather, there are peoples of different races. Do not let your genes, your culture, your very lives be "cooked" in the melting pot propaganda that has been dished out to you in extra servings and extra heaps than even you in your former state of mental slavery had appetite for! Do not let your White people be passed through the meat grinder of the phony patriotism, the "patriotism" that would have you ignore the greater bond of blood! For blood *is* thicker than water, even the waters surrounding one's country! Your race comes before any soil; your race comes before any society! And yes, your race comes before country too! This is the truth that makes mincemeat of the phony patriotism, the bright sun that turns the web of deceit into dust. Your true "us" has no border, certainly no border encompassing the multi-racial and the raceless! The patriotism of the future, dare I say it (!), will be the patriotism of the homogeneous ("same race") again, belief in a true fatherland because we are all Brothers and Sisters of the White Racial Family imbued with love for our father! Not a father of willy nilly bastards but rather of the racially legitimate! May we dare say also that the patriotism of the future, the love of patria ("fatherland"), will include salute to a flag that is also *racial*? Not a flag of merely pretty colors but a flag that also signifies *us*?

What a sweet word to the ear is that word "racial" to those who have rid their minds of the infection of so-called political correctness. For so long we have feared that word because we thought it implied that we had done something wrong but hadn't! For so long have we thought that seeing or hearing the word "racial" meant that we had mistreated somebody when all along we have been mistreating ourselves by *not* using the word! For so long we have avoided using the word at all costs, using proxies instead like "ethnic," "cultural," and the like that have made us feel safe from the ever-present guilt that we have supposedly incurred but *have not*! How often have we heard the admonition to not "bring race into this" or that topic when all along, race should have been the foundation, the backdrop, the overseer of everything! Race: the judge, jury, prosecution, and defense! White people are what we are, our race is what we are. Before we can figure out *who* we are as individuals we should at least feel the assurance of *what* we are, should we not? Before a child has thought about what he wants to be when he grows up, or even what he wants to be here and now, he already knows that he belongs to a particular family, *this* family. Why should it be any different with our race? We would not sacrifice our identification with our families; why should we sacrifice our identification with our race? This is *my* mother, this is *my* father, these are *my* siblings, and this is *my* race! No country can bear my identity more than my blood. No religion, which can be changed or ignored, can bear my identity more than my blood. No "income bracket," which can go up and down like a yo yo, can bear my identity more than my blood. It is my print and imprint, my cause and causing, my beginning and end. No artificiality bears a measure against it once true consciousness is awoken!

Dare we then to "bring race into this," that, and every other thing if such were not already automatic! Let us look at one of the most glaring examples of what is, was, and will be a racial issue in the United States and yet at the same time is denied to be such by our people, a denial as misguided and indeed downright silly as a drunk denying that booze is what is causing him to stumble down the stairs! I speak of the so-called "illegal immigration" problem which has been so pitifully reduced by the fearful (of that great word, Race) to be an anger based on illegality versus legality when all along the *true* aversion to millions of Mexicans, brown mestizoes invading the country has been *instinctual*, that well...they are brown! This has always been the real root of disgust at the illegal immigration problem but we have been afraid to say so because that would be "racist" or so the chorus of societal oppression utters. And yet, as thoroughly as our minds have been in chains, we still have had enough instinct, thankfully, to be disturbed by the thought that millions of non-whites have entered our habitat. Due to our emasculation though, we have groped elsewhere for an *explanation* of our discomfort other than that "horrible," "bigoted," and "discredited" sentiment of race. So what do we do? We don't want, deep within our psyche, these millions of brown people here but we have brainwashed ourselves into thinking that that is an immoral sentiment to have. So Eureka! We home in on the fact that the invaders broke the law in this society where a mania for "law" has overwhelmed a desire for what is true, right, and just and that certainly for White people as a people. However, were the Congress tomorrow to pass another law granting amnesty to all of the invaders as well as citizenship, would we be as content and happy that *that* law be obeyed as we are angry that the invaders broke the law coming here? Thus the law is in reality an excuse to oppose what we actually disdain for *racial* reasons: the proliferation of brown Mexicans in the country, an excuse because we think that race is "forbidden" to us! Thus we think it is fine to say that the millions of invaders broke the law and therefore should go home but we have been terrified like rabbits to say that the millions of *non-whites* should go home. "Law" has thus become yet another proxy for race, indeed one of the only proxies we have left. How eager we have been to proclaim our willingness to "defend the law" but how disdainful we have been to proclaim any willingness to "defend the best interests of our White race"! Why on earth though care whether the millions of non-white invaders are legal or illegal? The point is that they are here! If they were declared by law to be legal tomorrow, we *still* wouldn't want them here. Multitudes of White people came to America in generations past without any legal authorization but we didn't care because they were *White.* We are upset about the millions of non-white illegal immigrant invaders coming here because they are *not* White. We still have a residue of racial feeling, thank goodness! Our complaint that the invaders have broken the law has subsumed the real problem, that the invaders are not White! Blessed be the fact though that so many of us at least oppose the invasion even if we have deluded ourselves as to why!

For us who have broken the chains ensnaring our minds, whether something is "illegal" is no determinant of whether that something is *good.* Thus the non-white invasion of America could be as legal as blueberry pie—and in some cases is—but that hardly means that we should endorse it! A piece of paper with words on it declaring something to be illegal does not suddenly evoke our strenuous opposition, the lack of such words upon a piece of paper having our blessing! The problem with any invasion of a people not your own is that it is, um, an invasion of a people not of your own! Nothing more needs to be said! No apologies need to be made for our sentiment. There is no need to resort to the ruse of claiming that we are all in favor of (non-white) immigration just so long as it is "legal"! Whether the invaders are legal or illegal has never made a difference for the Congress could make them legal tomorrow and we would still not want them here. And if the complaint were really that the invaders broke the laws of Congress in the first place, shouldn't Congress be deemed the offended party entitled to forgive their wrong with another law granting amnesty if it so chose? In other words, if it is the breaking of a law that makes something bad, another law should be able to make it good. With the brown invasion though, nobody who opposes it is willing to accept that Congress could make things "good" with the passage of another law. Hence it is *not* the breaking of the law that is our true complaint!

Let us raze the weeds of false guilt that have grown awry within our conscience as to this problem and every other! The brown race is quite entitled to want more of its kind in America so as to increase its power and the White Race is quite entitled *not* to want more of the brown kind in America so as to prevent the *decrease* of *its* power. Thus speaks justice. For our White people, there exists no law that hurts our best interests which we can pronounce good and nor is any law good just because it is a law! And nor are actions that harm us bad because they break a law of some kind. Rather, actions are good or bad—like the brown invasion of America—on their own, depending upon whether they are good or bad for our White people! That is the only barometer that makes any sense if we are to let *any* laws determine our destiny. For otherwise, who do the laws serve exactly? We have become so enamored of legalism that we have forgotten that laws do not make anything wrong, right nor anything right, wrong. And that they can be the products of idiots as much as geniuses!

The mentally free White man happily finds *race* in the immigration (invasion) problem; he has no need to "bring race into it" for it is already there! How he shuns the denials, the hypocrisy, the defensiveness, the window dressing of the "I just want the laws to be followed" mantra, the excuse others find socially acceptable enough to utter, the readily-available rain cloud whenever a deluge of falsehood is desired! Happily he tells the truth to himself and to others if they will only hear him; "there are too many Mexicans here already" bears no sting, no shame, no guilt requiring a salve, an erasure, or a cleansing but rather is a love of self to laud and applaud! And he reserves the right unto himself to wash the ears of others if he must! His country is his garden as far as he is concerned and who ever heard of a gardener being a slave to whatever plants wish to take up residence there, law or no law? And who ever heard of a gardener fearful of calling this plant this and that plant that and discriminating with his love and disdain?

All laws must be for us, must serve us, and must be for our

own best interests as a people, White people! Therein dwells their justice, their wisdom, and their respect. Otherwise they are mere pieces of paper peddled forth by those without claim to any wisdom or loyalty. So different is that demand from what we have today where absolutely *no* law is promulgated or expected to serve our best interests as a people! And that is called "progress"? We instead call that regress of a most foul sort, a subversion of the entire purpose of law which is to complement the impulse of all Nature. And what is the impulse of all Nature that we can see all around us, if we only look? Benefit the best interests of your own kind! Nature provides this impulse to all its creatures and it is the task of the laws of men to see that impulse through in all of their particulars. That in a few words is the point of all law: Man's laws fulfill Nature's law. This is the hope of the future, your future, if the mere laws of men could ever deserve the appellation of "hope"! For the hopes of a White people whose minds are no longer in chains are grander than any laws! How truly today there is much talk of laws and so little of hopes, so many debates about laws and so few about hopes. And do not our White people deserve hopes of their own? Should we allow any laws to crush our hopes? Blessed will be our people when the day comes when instead of allowing laws to crush our hopes that all of the laws will *serve* our hopes! A man is not a piece of paper and a piece of paper does not make a man! Blessed will be the day when the arbitrary laws of governments will no longer be allowed to crush our hopes, when instead the laws of the present will wilt before their flame!

The youth, especially, know that tomorrow need not be like today. There is no path of eggshells that they fear traversing for fear of upsetting rotten eggs! Their will is their command, not the stone tablets of yesterday that were already brittle when they were being etched. How joyous the youth will find it to say yea! to that which their elders (currently) demand a nay! How distasteful, how discontent will they be with the phony equality dogma whose drink they once imbibed. What better way to rebel, what better way to revolt, than to be racial in the sea of the raceless, the periscope amidst the quarry, the lightning bolt in the field of drab! For make no mistake my young Brothers and Sisters, there is no dynamism in the status quo, there is no revolution in reaction, and there is no idealism in emulating your parents! You need not be their clones, and you need not carry their pitchers of water. If their minds remain in chains, yours need not be alongside, and if they demand of themselves that they remain passive anvils, you on the other hand can be hammers, hammerers of the future! Let them forage while you forge. Let them chide while you chisel. Let them wring their hands while you wring a future out of tomorrow! A future for your race!

There is strength within you. Is there enough strength to break your own chains with your bare hands? There is strength within you, but would you let that strength be dissipated through passive transfixture to technological fantasies of fiction instead of being your raw, assertive, natural selves? For that is what is happening today with so many. Life has lost its sting but also its charm, its bitterness but also its sweetness, perhaps its solitariness but also its fulfillment. Would you get these back? Can you shut off the boob tube and feel your own power? Can you separate the wheat from the chaff in a society with far more of the latter than the former?

You have been bombarded with images designed to degrade you as a White man or woman. Trashy music, books, and general "entertainment" have been promoted to you in order to turn you away from your own kind, your own nature, your own culture, your own meaning! Tear down these false idols, my Brothers and Sisters! Tear down the posters of Negroes from your walls, the false idols of your former propagandized selves! Trample the disks of decadence, the thumping cacophony of the Negro mind that has been foisted upon you as if there were never an alternative! Rip to shreds the depictions of the sisters of your race as mere pieces of flesh to be salivated at, the debasement of those who give life! Restore the White woman to her place of respect and appreciation, that which she had before our minds were enchained. Restore respect for your people who have been the victims of such assault. Make bonfires of the decadence so as to release a new spirit! The spirit of White racial love and value. The spirit of White racial excellence and honor. There are no heroes outside of our own race. There is no homage to be paid outside of our own race. There is no culture to be adhered to outside of our own race. No Negro who can dribble a basketball is worthy of your adulation. No Negro poetry interspersed with profanity and the grabbing of crotches deserves your affection! Rid your hearts and minds of such trash fully and return to the bosom of your own people. The only "(w)rapper" belongs under your shoe! You know you are better than that. Your race did not send rockets to the moon so that you could wallow in the muck. Your race did not produce a Shakespeare so that you could embrace perverts. Your natural greatness does not willingly coincide with degeneracy and thus one of them must go! Separate your wheat from the chaff of worthlessness. Recognize that no creation should be created that is unworthy of its creator, that creation is the prerogative of the superior, not the mass and not the inferior! That the creative and "equality" do *not* go hand in hand! We have our own culture and it is rich enough that we need not be paupers at the doors of the mud huts of others. We have our own heroes whose great number could never be calculated even if we spent all of our hours trying. Why then reach within *another* race in search of heroes, my brethren? We have music the most exalted that could be conceived. Why opt instead for "music" that would return us to the caves or to the trees? It took so many eons for us to leave them, after all!

Do not confuse the pizzazz of technology for substance. Know that there is more greatness in a sublime thought than in a graphic, a word than in a gesture, and enlightenment than in a light show. We are bombarded with images but almost nothing of substance, a cackle of noise but almost nothing of melody, a thumping of barbarism but almost nothing of beauty...and it is not only of music of which I speak! Alas no one has been willing to say so because of the equality virus, the equality infection that has ailed us so. Equality is the arch poisoner, the arch leveler of that which stands upon tall peaks and the raiser of that which is subterranean. "Equality" claims that all is of equal value—to *someone*, anyway! Equality offers a suitable perversion for every vice. Equality renders men cattle. Equality prevents our people from feeling a sense of shame for their debasing themselves; equality offers an excuse for every weakness. Equality would discourage a man from proclaiming that he is better than his fellows even though he has proven it time and again; thus he climbs up the muddy hill only to slip down again. Equality causes a man to consent to the lowering of himself. For if men were really equal to one another, why *shouldn't* every choice made by men also be of equal worth, and if every choice were of equal worth, why should there be any shame in pursuing the most abysmal ones? Thus we as White people have lost our sense of scorn for the inferior but it is precisely a sense of scorn for the inferior that keeps a race superior! We would never have allowed and countenanced our habits, our tastes, our very mentality to be nigrified otherwise. For if we start from the position that all men are equal, created or otherwise, all choices by those men must also be of equal value even if we don't consciously conclude such. *Real* trash is given a forum and its incessant promotion in the media dupes our people, especially our youth, into thinking that there is actually value in the trash when there isn't. Thus have we lowered ourselves, my Brothers and Sisters! Thus have we gone from Shakespeare to (c)rap, from marveling at a Michelangelo to Michael Jackson, and to thinking that a ball stuffed into a basket is a real triumph! Rid yourself of such trash; pull up the roots of your debasement! Do not step an inch outside your true culture, that culture that flows naturally from your unique racial existence. Youth! Turn off the boob tube; no longer let yourself be the subject of manipulation. Do not let yourself be enshrouded with a cloth not of your own, ways not of your own, manners not of our own. Rid the fungi from your brain, the despoilment from your tongue! It makes no more sense for you to embrace the culture of another race than for a cardinal to grow blue feathers. You are White and thus your culture is the same. There is a reason why a

Beethoven wrote symphonies while the people of Africa slapped at bongo drums: the culture of each was the outgrowth of its identity!

My Brothers and Sisters, you will not be great again until the "equality" virus has withered in your soul and the spirit of hierarchy has been reborn, the spirit of distinction between all things involving man. Alas though, maybe you do not wish to be great and are content to be mediocre? Content to be interchangeable with everyone else? Content to be shell rather than substance, wrapping rather than gift? Is this what we have been reduced to? Not deep within you, I say, for such is not your nature! It is in your nature to love personality, to love wit, to love uniqueness, to love success, to love variety, to love diversity—all things that represent the unequal! For inequality is the law of life and you still love life!

We White people should not apologize for our success and nor do we owe anyone but ourselves. We do not owe the other races our food, our clothes, our technology or anything else and if they suffer due to the lack of our largesse, that is their fault, not ours! Rid yourself of the idea that it is your duty, White Brother and Sister, to take care of the welfare of the other races when they should be taking care of themselves! If they have too many children for themselves to take care of, how is that your fault? If they don't know how to plant crops, how is that your fault? If they abuse their land so that it no longer bears fruit, how is that your fault? See where the equality lie has affected your decisions? You have feverishly sought to raise up "the needy," "the underprivileged," "the downtrodden" non-white races in part because the thought has been in the back of your mind that "all men are equal" and thus are entitled to some kind of relatively equal life! All the while your own White people have scrimped and saved, denied the largesse that you have given to others! While we have fed and clothed the other races, many of our own people have had empty bellies and have gone in need of clothes. While we have caused the rapid increase in numbers of the non-whites due to our largesse, the number of our own White people on this earth has shrunk! White couples everywhere forgo having children because they feel hard pressed to afford it while non-whites, with their largesse courtesy of White people in hand, are under no such coercion. They can breed willy nilly while we "defer" having children. If there is any largesse to be given, let it be to our own people! End the insanity of causing the proliferation of the non-whites so that they can crowd us off of the earth! This is what is happening before your eyes. White people feed the non-whites and the non-whites breed. Our wombs are barren while that of the non-whites are overflowing. Not one stalk of wheat should be placed into their hands. Not one tablet of medicine. Your duty is to your own people instead! If you wish to be charitable, be charitable to your own people. There are, after all, plenty of White people who are poor to be helped! See to it that our White couples can have all of the children that they desire, putting money into your *own* people's hands rather than squandering it elsewhere! And in fact make the day also come when a father and husband will be able to provide for his entire family with *one* paycheck once again! And oppose the theft of our resources by governments! Such is treason to us. No government over White people has the right to take money that would feed *us*, clothe *us*, treat *us* and give it to the other races so as to feed *them*, clothe *them*, and treat *them*! Such is an abomination, as selective as we may be in the use of such a word. White people across America lose their homes for lack of money because their money is taken from them and given to the non-whites so that *they* can build homes! White people forsake having children while the non-whites have children with *their* money! End this wrong of our times!

The wise race is the race that looks after its own best interests; the foolish race is the race that concerns itself with the best interests of the others. Have we not been foolish long enough, my Brothers and Sisters? Where is the sense in allowing our presence on this earth to turn into absence, our voices into echoes, our footsteps into fossils? Where is the sense in making way for the other races who already inhabit too much of the world as it is? Where is the sense in always being generous with what we have until we no longer have it? Are we men or are we lemmings? Why must we always be the ones to vacate what is ours, scampering away under the myth that the other races have a right to it or a right to our misplaced kindness? On the other hand, when have you ever heard of a non-white neighborhood becoming *White*, a non-white majority country becoming more *White*, Africa becoming more *White*, Asia becoming more *White*, South America becoming more *White*? Instead it is *always the other way around*, always *us* having to make way, always *us* on the way out, always *America and Europe* darkening, always *our* dispossession!

But surely I digress, surely I say what you already know? Surely the chains of your (former) mental slavery no longer clank loudly enough to drown out your clear discernment of the world around you? Surely you realize that feeding the hungry children of Africa only results in...more hungry children of Africa and ultimately those children of Africa looking covetously upon America and Europe (and Canada and Australia, for that matter) as an alluring new home away from their own crowded, destitute continent? Surely you realize that subsidizing "the disadvantaged" only results in more "disadvantaged" to contend with due to your own previous misplaced altruism? Surely you realize that if you as White people do not yourselves have children to inhabit the land that the non-whites will feel entitled to inhabit it instead? Surely you realize that when you dispense resources to the other races, you are withholding them from your own? That when you are building new schools in Afghanistan, you are *not* building those schools for White people? That when you are feeding the other races, you are denying your own race that very food? That when your heartstrings are being pulled for non-whites, they are not being pulled for your own people? Surely you realize that pouring Africans, Mexicans, and Asians into America and Europe inevitably means that America and Europe will look more like Africa, Mexico, and Asia? That America and Europe, in other words, will look more and more like those hellholes? Surely you realize that if you do not look out for your own best interests as White people, the other races will not come to the rescue and do it for you, that they do not share the misplaced altruism with which you have been afflicted?

But alas, those who wield power over our people today assume that the mental slavery of our people is permanent! Thus they say that America will "irreversibly" be a majority non-white country in the near future, that various countries in Europe will "inevitably" be majority Muslim (non-white) in so many years, and the like. They count on your subjugation, your supplication, your feebleness, your limp-wristedness in perpetuity! They count on you to keep sacrificing your culture, your territory, your genes, even your very lives for the melting pot travesty that results in the annihilation of everything you are! And who can blame them? Their propaganda is firmly in the saddle, their manipulation firmly in perpetual application, so why should their prognosis for the future *not* coincide with the present idiocy?

There can only be the following answer to that: a rise in White consciousness despite all of their best efforts, a rise in the feeling that White people have given up too much already in obeisance to the propaganda machine, a sickening and tiring of the myths we have been taught, a realization that we are a dwindling minority that *cannot* count on the altruism of the other races the same way that they have counted on ours. A rising White consciousness, that is the only way, for the racially suicidal thoughts that have put our people in the horrible situation in which they find themselves today can only be countered with those thoughts that can defeat them!

As the White liberal might say, "Having a few Hispanics in our community was pretty neat and I was thrilled with the 'diversity,' but now that they are a majority and the community has become a barrio with those with White skin like me feeling unwelcome, I'm leaving!" In other words, the propaganda of White sacrifice is starting to wear thin, is starting to lose its effectiveness due to the changing situation in which White people increasingly find themselves as well as due to its sheer staleness.

"Diversity" doesn't seem so pleasant when *White* people are the minority. The so-called "fairness" of today doesn't seem to make much sense anymore when it so obviously means "White people, make way!" The so-called "equality" of today doesn't seem to make sense anymore when it so obviously means "White people, you lose!" The so-called "diversity" of today doesn't seem to make much sense anymore when it so obviously means the weeds *overtaking* the garden. We will see though, my Brothers and Sisters! So many thoughts and actions have become habitual for you, indeed addictive, that even when you see parts of the truth, the whole may be missed, or even when your thoughts have been liberated from the chains that bound them, your actions do not follow. So much has been invested in the lies upon the axis of which the present society spins, so much assumed, so much taken for granted. And yet when full consciousness *has* been achieved, the chains of our previous befuddlement fall away like the lifeless dead weight that they are!

You know that even with the minds of our people in chains that there is still much pretentiousness, so much saying of things that we do not really believe just to accommodate the mantra! Do White people really believe, for example, that blacks are our intellectual equals or have we been saying that, when the question is rarely asked (and the question is rarely asked because somebody might answer the 'wrong' way), because we are expected to? Do White people *really* believe, for example, that "the only difference between the races is the color of their skin" or do we say that, once again, because that is the expected answer that has been pounded into our consciousness from all sides? Do White people *really* believe that there is no moral problem with racial intermarriage (mongrelization) or do we just say that, especially to pollsters, because to say otherwise is to risk being assailed as a "racist"? Are we really all just tickled pink to see a mongrel child in a baby carriage when we were figuring on seeing a child that looks like his mother? What fine actors we have become! And even when the curtain has been drawn and the stage lights have been turned off, we still act—to ourselves. We deserve an academy award for our performances because we can so successfully suppress what we are really feeling, feelings that no chains upon our minds can fully restrict. It is George Orwell's *1984*. We believe but we don't believe. We say but we don't say. We either truly deny or we are in denial. We put the face on which society expects us to evince and we forget whether it is flesh or plastic. We seek to do what society has proclaimed to be "good" because we think it will raise our esteem in the opinion of our fellows rather than because we truly, deep down, consider the act "good." Thus we have worked hard to assist the other races because it has been *expected* of us! The good news, though, is that it is not so hard to veer *expectations* in a different direction. A slight recalculation here, a little adjustment there, and the expectation is no longer the same and the expectations of the past take on the character in our eyes of cruel, absurd follies!

We want to "feed the children"? Wonderful. There are plenty of White children needing to be fed good, nutritious food instead of the junk food with which they are presently inundated. We want to build schools? Wonderful. There are many schools where White children are presently studying that are crumbling that can be rebuilt much better than they were built to begin with. We want to treat disease? Wonderful. There are millions of White people with diabetes, cancer, heart disease, Alzheimer's, and innumerable other ailments that could use the many billions of dollars for treatment that is likewise currently being wasted on the other races. We want to build roads? Wonderful. There are innumerable roads where White people drive that need their potholes filled up and there are plenty of places where White people live that need roads to begin with. We want children to get a better education? Wonderful. We can finally increase the salaries of our White teachers who are teaching our White students rather than, as always, squandering the money on the people of Africa, Asia, and South America and on stupid wars that cost trillions. We want to be all around wealthier, happier, and secure as a people? Wonderful! All we have to do is keep our money within our own race! Thus the altruism remains! It is simply redirected to our own people. Our *own* flowers bloom. Our *own* buds bear fruit. Our *own* higher potential is reached. Is that really something to regret? Is that really something to despise? A people takes care of self. How grand it is to rejoin every other living creature on this earth! The expectation becomes, "you are White and therefore you, in your beneficence, in your altruism, in your good works, will help your fellow White people and there is always plenty of help that is needed!"

After all, who ever came up with the idea that every White person owns a castle complete with a moat? Who ever came up with the idea that we are all swimming in cash, that we all have so much money that if we don't get rid of it on the other races, we will drown? Who ever came up with the idea that we should ignore the needs, or even the desires for that matter, of our own people in favor of that of the other races? If the other races cannot feed themselves, that is their own hard luck: if they would quit having so many children, they wouldn't have that problem just as White people have reduced their *own* poverty by limiting their family size. In other words, we presently are subsidizing large non-white families when we don't even subsidize our own families. We forgo having children of our own due to lack of money while money is siphoned off from our own people and given to the other races so that *they* can have children. Where is the sense in that? Where is the morality? Tell the White woman who has had her tubes tied for *financial* reasons that the resources she could have had to support more children should instead be diverted to Africa, Asia, and South America. Tell the White woman who is *forced* to work outside the home in order for the family to make its ends meet that the resources *that would prevent that* should be spent in other countries on other races. Tell the White man who ruined his health working in coal mines or with asbestos that he is undeserving of the help that is instead diverted to the other races. Where are the "celebrities" for them? Do we not have sadness and suffering within our own racial household? Our White people have *never* been so well off to have wanted to throw their money at the other races, to have denied themselves!

We have needs, we have wants, and it really doesn't matter which is which but rather that *we* fulfill them! Turn the channel when the sob stories come on about the hungry non-whites when there are White people who are hungry, when there are White families in hard, desperate straits, when there are White people who have unfulfilled hopes and dreams! And demand that the governments of the world stop taxing us to support the other races! No more billions per year going here, there, and everywhere to races not our own. We have much to do within our own race, much suffering to alleviate, many minds to cultivate, many buildings to renovate, and a people to propagate! No more of the other races feeding at our trough! No more calling ourselves "humanitarians" for subsidizing the other races while our own suffers, while our own goes without! The so-called "developing world" has had plenty of chance to develop already. Now is the time to develop our own. White men and women, give nothing whatever to the other races but rather to your own people. We have so much to do for ourselves!

The world is no longer what it was. Our disregard for our racial identity, loyalty, and best interests has resulted in a world in which we are now less than five hundred million of the seven billion on earth. The fact that the so-called "population explosion" has been an entirely non-white explosion has been conveniently omitted from society's discussion. Due to our subsidy and our influence, the other races now also possess great wealth of their own with which they can take care of their own less fortunate. There are African leaders, for example, who are multi-millionaires and indeed billionaires so let *them* take care of their own people! They possess the richest continent on earth in raw materials and China, India, and Brazil are growing economic powerhouses. Why then must it always be the door of White people that is beaten down for resources?

There is much perversity in the world but know that there is nothing more perverse than the mongrelization of your blood. Does it not go without saying that we who believe in White Life must oppose such genocide ("race killing") with every fiber of our being? Rid your mind of the idea that anyone has the "right" to kill your race! For there is no more right to kill us through mongrelization any more than there is through bullets! Better in fact would it be were we to lose our racial life through a hail of bullets than through the contamination of stock! For while biological death is natural, genetic death is not! This is the wisdom of eternity instead of the frivolousness of the moment, the love of the continuing race over the transitory individual. We know of that which our instincts speak, the yearning for obedience to Nature's law of racial purity and hence of preservation! Let us accept that we are instinctively sickened at the sight of racial mongrelization! Let us say that that which goes against Nature is perverse no matter *what* intellectual trappings are attached to it! The sick feeling in our stomachs at the sight of mongrelization is the conscience of our race speaking, a conscience that says that we behold death in living form! It is a conscience that cries out for salvation from such self-inflicted genocide! And yet we have for too long stifled those cries, instead proceeding to convince ourselves that *we* are in the wrong! We are not, Brothers and Sisters! Our racial conscience is not wrong, our instincts do not lie, and our guts do not need reeducation. Rather our education must conform to our guts! Mongrelization means the end of White Life; thus all mongrelization must instead be ended. The matter is crystal clear and simple just as all truths are. There is no such thing as valuing White Life and tolerating the destruction of that life. You either value White Life or you do not in your tolerance of its destruction!

A race has a right to seek to preserve its life and any supposed "right" of an individual to destroy that life withers before it. Let us say plainly: your genes are not yours alone! They belong to your race as leaves to a tree! No woman of our race has a right to give birth to destroyed-race babies any more than she has a right to kill her own *White* babies. Both are acts of destruction. The second act is murder; the first is genocide ("race-killing"), literally. Genocide doesn't somehow become right when it happens to be our White Race that is being killed! There is a reason why the mixing of our blood with that of the other races was always considered immoral until recently: it was! There is a reason why the majority of the United States up until the 1960s outlawed the marriage of different races: because such a thing was rightly viewed as a cancer that would eat away at our racial life! It is not that the past was too racial but that it was not racial enough! It is not that there were laws aimed at our preservation that was the problem but rather that there were not enough of them, that they were not strong enough, and that they were capable of being overthrown! Better to drip with race than to be a desert, better to be fanatical for race than to sanction genocide! And what is the violation of Nature's law of racial exclusivity, racial purity but genocide masqueraded as "love"? Let us say that such a so-called "love" is rather a will to annihilation, rather an act of *hate*! And may your love for your race conquer such hate, my Brothers and Sisters!

And do not, once again, let the laws of today's misbegotten societies determine your right and wrong! The so-called Supreme Court of the United States, for example, can declare all it wants that a State does not have a "compelling interest" in keeping the White Race White but we who love the life of our race know that mere words on paper cannot wipe out that which is naturally true and right! No law of men can hold a candle to the laws of Nature! And we Racial Loyalists, White Lovers, would rather doubt instead whether the Supreme Court *itself* has a compelling reason to exist! No ink on a piece of paper can overrule a race's right to seek its preservation, the only "right" that exists inherently in this world! No law issued by individual men can ever trump Nature's eternal laws! The perversions that afflict the misbegotten societies of today stem in part from the bizarre idea that White people do not have a compelling interest in preserving themselves. Reject this idea utterly, my Brothers and Sisters! Confront and rebuke all annihilations of your race! Fight the genocide that is amongst us and defeat it utterly. The individual's genes are not only his! He has no right to kill them, to warp them, to distort them. He has no right to create beings that violate Nature's law of racial purity, racial exclusivity. He has no right to create beings whose loyalties are divided by virtue of their very birth, beings of mixed race and hence of mixed loyalties and mixed identity! No woman has the right to spread her legs for an individual of another race; better that she herself be destroyed than her eternal bloodline! This is the will to life of a race, our race. We assert our life as a race or we die as a race. There is no in-between. May both conscience and consciousness stir in your soul; may both love and loyalty to your blood be inextricably linked in your heart! If you feel hostility to the genocide around you, it is because you must. If you do not smile at the destruction of your kind through mongrelization, it is because your racial conscience forbids it! Do not replace that conscience with conformity, your frown with flippancy! Your racial conscience is the good one; it is the raceless conscience that has been foisted upon you that is the one that is bad! Our wombs are for our weal; our seed is for our soil. Such is the law of life, a law that fully deserves your love! Understand that multiracial societies are anti-Nature, anti-instinct, and anti-survival and that they are the facilitators of genocide in the 21st century! Races can be killed through violence and races can be killed through disease but they can also be killed through their mixing with other races. The struggle to end such genocide is the pro-life movement of the 21st century.

You have been told not to scrutinize matters from a racial perspective but you have only been taught this so as to disempower your people. Of course you should think racially, because you are indeed part of a race! Does not the lion act in terms of what is good for lions? Does not even the humble ant act in terms of what is good for his particular race of ant to which he belongs? Do red ants allow black ants into their holes? Do honey bees allow bumble bees into their hives? They and all other creatures possess a racial conscience and so do you! You have a right to fight for your own habitat; you have a right to fight for your own best interests! You have a right to exclude that which is not of your own kind from *your* society; you have a right not to be color-blind! Walk down your racial path and do not veer. Replace the guilty conscience with the racial conscience, the conscience of weakness with the conscience of strength! Replace the guilty conscience with the racial conscience, the conscience of defeat with the conscience of victory! Replace the guilty conscience with the racial conscience, the conscience of death with the conscience of life! Even if your race were the worst race that there ever was, it would still compel your allegiance. Even if your race really did to the other races what the peddlers of guilt want you to believe it did, namely subjugate, pillage, or whatever, it still deserves your love! Let a thousand massacres be laid at its door; let us underwrite them all rather than hang our heads in shame for the deeds of our ancestors who gave us life! May the apologies come to an end; may our heads be held high! May the racial conscience flower forth with unencumbered fragrance, may our dawn eject the present night! A people rises from its calloused knees to its squarely planted feet! For this I yearn, the inevitable result of the freeing of our minds from chains and the intellectualisms that would divert us from the path so distinctly laid out for us by the natural world around us. Within our breasts, within our nerves, within our vision is the racial conscience that only need be heeded, the conscience that commands: be for your Race, always. Better to separate ourselves from the present society than from our racial conscience. Better to rock the rotten boat of today and swim instead for a pristine shore! You who have broken the chains of your mental slavery are not the ones whose souls are dissonant; rather you are the ones capable of true harmony!

You, my fellow lovers of White Life, must show a courage of which you did not know yourselves capable. You must not only defy the tablets of your former mental slavery, and which enslave your brethren still, but you must also defy your own will to comfort and contentedness that would suck you back into that which you thought you had overcome! For the chains of our former mental slavery, even though broken, may still weigh us down while resting upon our feet! Better to fling them as far away as we can, to remember that while a mind may be free, we may still be bogged down by chains that linger upon our feet or even by

136

muzzles upon our mouths. If you, my Brother or Sister, now have love for your race but are afraid to voice it for fear of the wrath of those whose minds are still in chains, for example, do you not still have fetters about you that are oppressing your true nature, your true spirit, and your true duty? For love entails a duty, my brethren, and such a duty cannot be fulfilled through silence of words and silence of deeds! You must speak even when there are daggered teeth and snarls against you. You must speak even when you seemingly stand alone! Into the dens of the mangy curs you must traverse, their saliva dripping with hate and envy at your racial freedom! They may even nip at you from time to time, hoping to infect you with their decadence! And yet persevere you must, a shining, admired light must you be, a flame that would sear the shackles of the mangy so that they may become men again!

Return to the natural world from which you have been divorced for so long. Value your instincts before all intellectualisms and that which is yours before that which belongs to others. What is yours has value that you need not explain; what is yours has value precisely because it is indeed yours! The facts of life come before all books of whim; the foundation comes before all that which is built upon it! The sun shines upon race here, there, and everywhere but doesn't shine upon a single thought; is it not true that before a single man was ever imprisoned in a dungeon, men were already prisoners of their own minds? Do not be prisoners of your own minds, my Brothers and Sisters! Love the physical world!

We whose minds are not fettered, not in chains, know the machinations of the present society! We know the guilty conscience that it attempts to foist upon us for doing nothing other than wanting to love the natural world! How the haters of that world wish to force us down to bended knee, how they wish that we would divest ourselves of our spines! All in obeisance to their artificial, "multicultural," *mongrel* society that they have the strange idea will last forever! But Brothers and Sisters, we know it will not! We know that though the masses can be led against their own instincts for a long time—(dreadfully long as we know!)—the day will come when those instincts will reassert themselves, specifically the instinct for racial self-preservation and for the homogeneous society! We know that even in the midst of the propaganda with which we are saturated, our instincts remain. They simply must be unleashed, unfurled, buds that are allowed to flower. Have we not as White people been nipped in the bud long enough? Has not our spirit been squelched in its cradle long enough? The day is coming, my Brothers and Sisters, when that madness will come to an end! We grow tired of the pruning shears nipping away at our natural selves, and the pruner grows tired of the pruning! There is far more work involved in suppression than there is in the freedom of our naturally racial selves and the moment the suppression grows weary is the moment our racial selves burst forth with all of their grandeur, innocence, and love. It is already happening now. The more entrenched the mongrel society becomes, the more we feel the stirring of our instincts against it. The more we are told as a people that we must bow, the more our instincts rebel at the thought! We can only defy those instincts for so long; their reassertion is coming. Like all tyrannies of artifice, of the artificial, the mongrel society lives on borrowed time because it is in the true nature of every living creature on this earth to want to live in a society of its own kind. This nature has never left us no matter how much propaganda has been meted out to us and nor will it leave us in the future when that propaganda has long since become despised. Propaganda comes and goes but the instincts remain! Indeed, what is the propaganda of the "multiracial," mongrel society but a thought and when has a mere thought ever outlasted the instincts that are rooted in our very being? Thus our instincts for our own kind shall outlast the machinations of the present order; they shall march on long after the mongrel society that the machinations assert and protect shall have become brittle and passed into dust!

Even today, the word "mongrel" remains a distasteful word to us all because it represents, *to our instincts*, a distasteful fact, a distasteful being! Otherwise why would use of that word even now cause people to feel offense? We who would laud pure breed dogs and horses, why should we not want pure breed men as well and indeed a society itself that believes in purity? Indeed, the purity we want is so much higher than that of any animal; would that we would have that much more determination for it! Should we not have more consideration for whom we ourselves breed with than the partners whom we assign to our *animals*? Are our animals of such greater worth than ourselves that we should instead only care about whether *their* breeding is worthy? May our own genes be more important to us than the genes of animals! May we decline the current hodgepodge society with which we are afflicted and build one instead that is conducive to our own well-being! May we walk out from under the guilty conscience cloud that we did not conjure up nor deserve! The guilty conscience cloud that would discourage us from doing that which is best for our own people. The guilty conscience cloud that would attempt to deny us our own best interests. The guilty conscience cloud that would deny us our own voting bloc. The guilty conscience cloud that would even dare to deny us our own future as an extant people!

We ask ourselves: do the Chinese feel guilty for having an overwhelmingly yellow society? Do the Nigerians ("niggers") feel guilty for having an overwhelmingly black society? Do the Israelis feel guilty for having an overwhelmingly Jewish society? No? Then why should White people feel guilty for wanting to have a White society, overwhelmingly or otherwise? Why should we feel guilty for loving ourselves, for asserting ourselves, for disdaining any and all things that are bad for ourselves? How could such sentiments ever be deemed as "extreme," "radical," "hateful," or the like as claimed by the present society? Far be it from us to tell the black man that he shouldn't care about black people. Far be it from us to tell the yellow man that he shouldn't care about yellow people. Far be it from us to tell the brown man that he shouldn't care about brown people. Far be it from us to tell Jews that they shouldn't care about fellow Jews and have a State devoted to their preservation, in fact. Somehow though things are expected to be different for us *White* people, that we are expected to walk off of the gangplank of history and with a smile to boot! The question for us, indeed the *only* question for us in the end, is *whether we will acquiesce.* Though our instincts will always be with us, that does not necessarily mean that we will be around to implement them! For the mongrel society longs for our destruction culturally, genetically, and maybe even biologically before the reassertion of our instincts has taken place! That is the race against time in which we find ourselves; will we win that race, *our* race, or lose it miserably? Will we refuse to see our race broken up, overwhelmed, pilfered, pillaged, and polluted out of existence? For that is the inevitable result of the "multiracial" society, the mongrel society, if left unchecked: mongrel people! Will we today refuse to go the route of the White people of India, the White people of Egypt, and even the White people of America and China, yes, who thousands of years ago found themselves submerged and eliminated in a sea of color in those places? For their instincts did not assert themselves in time or if they did, it was too late to prevent their demise in any case since they were outnumbered so vastly! And now how many people even know that our White people did indeed populate these places at all at one time? That White people are *indigenous* to western China and Egypt? That White people *preceded* the "American" Indians to the North American continent? That the well-known caste system of India was, less well-known, created to preserve the genes of the White people there? Why *didn't* you know, you ask? You didn't know these things because we *lost* in those places! Even our very languages became extinct. Do you want to see now White people everywhere likewise be buried in the dust, a mere archeological find for the non-white races in the future? Will these non-whites one day marvel that there was ever a race that did not exclusively have black hair and brown eyes like them but instead had variety, diversity, and uniqueness? Will they one day marvel that there was ever a race that had eyes the color of the heavens and hair the color of a sunset, eyes the color of meadows and hair the color of flax? What value we have in ourselves if we would only appreciate it! And rally now, today, for that value! No mere animal deserves the attention we should give to ourselves. No beauty should capture our eyes in *lieu* of our own! Do you really wish to sanction a day when through the course of cultural, genetic, and biological annihilation, there are no longer any natural blondes on this earth, no longer anyone with green, gray, or blue eyes, no longer a single redhead, no longer anybody but the drab, cookie-cutter colored races devoid of your qualities? And yet that is the result of the mongrel society, the whittling away of our distinction, the whittling away of our beauty, the whittling away of our uniqueness, the whittling away of our life. If there is an hourglass of our race's existence that is running out of sand, the thing to do is *turn it over*, not merely gawk at it or ignore it! Subvert the hourglass, my Brothers and Sisters! Make the sand of your existence run the *other* way. Sound the death knell not of your own existence, no, but rather of the mongrel society! Proclaim indeed that *its* time has been borrowed, not yours! Show that your instincts have returned, the chains upon your minds forever broken and indeed melted down so as to form your shield and sword for your own kind! Joyous is your purity reasserted, bad is the canker and cancer of the mongrel society! Do not, now worldwide, go the route of your brethren of the past in various places but rather learn from their misfortune so as to avoid your own! Hold a torch to that which decays, degrades, and defames your kind while lighting the way to a society where the sand of your existence *never* runs out, to a society of your eternity!

"A society of our eternity"...can we dare to look that far ahead? A society of our being, can we dare to envision it? What attachments to the present one that we would not deign to forgo, what disease for which we would not prefer a cure? Some of us though have lived in the mongrel society for so long that it has become a sort of "normal" for us! And like a drug addict who has been deprived of his poison, we may well experience a withdrawal! Let it come, if it must, for we know that we are better off without the poison in the long run. Let it come, if it must, for we know that poison is incompatible with life, our life. The mass media culture has drugged us long enough, has convinced us of a supposed normalcy that does not exist, that of the "multiracial" (mongrel) society. How it has paraded the non-white cast of characters before our eyes, how it has longed to convince us that we and the other races are oh so interchangeable! Of course we have experienced some addiction, the boob tube having been such a huge part of all of our lives. Of course ending that addiction may not be entirely pleasant, but what ending of addiction is? Sever the tentacles of your addiction to the mongrel society, my Brothers and Sisters! Realize that your supposed need to behold the other races of men within your society has been artificially induced! Realize that there is no such thing as a *natural* multiracial society for Nature herself despises such things, that no where among the non-domesticated creatures of her realm does such a thing exist! Realize that there is no yearning for multiracialism that is not artificial, that there is no love for multiracialism that is not the product of the propaganda that was imposed upon us, injected into us, through our television sets, the injection of a poison into our psyche! Veins are not the only receptacles of poison, after all, nor even the worst ones! Had there never been television, there never would have been any particular regard for multiracialism. And even today, were television to cease to exist, all regard for multiracialism would quickly follow suit! For that was the conduit for your manipulation, my Brothers and Sisters! You were bombarded with images of those not of your own race and thus of course the multiracial, mongrel society seemed "normal" to you! Your thoughts followed the images; your world was created for you through a boob tube! And today those of our people, our race, our kind who are filled to the brim with hate for what we lovers of White Life love, only harbor that hate because of their manipulation through the screens of their living rooms, their bedrooms, their kitchens, and elsewhere! Expose the manipulation, my brethren! Counter the images of artificiality with the indications of Nature, the momentary perversion with the normal course of history, the laws of a director's chair with the laws of life!

We are the preservers, not the destroyers. We understand that *all* forms of destruction of our race are bad and not just those through physical violence or disease. We understand that to love the life of a race is to love its *whole* life, not just whether the hearts still literally beat in our chests, but also that our White Race *itself* continue to live and that our White culture—the collection of cultures of the White peoples of the world—also continues to live. This is full life and its preservation, not the mere prevention of destruction of individual lives. Just as we all have individual family trees, we also have a racial family tree that we should not want chopped down. Banish from your psyche the notion that there is any such thing as a "human race" for such a thing does not exist! There is instead our race and there are the other races. They are not us and we are not them. Their dreams are all too often our nightmares. The dream of a so-called "colorblind" society is the dream for annihilation, the destruction of identity that is always the result of the mingling of the different races. Hail instead your White identity! But you already know that my Brothers and Sisters! But now your task is to make all of your brethren know it too! Your vision is your continued identity; your calling is the continued flow of your blood, your culture, your life as a people. Your foe is that which would end your continued identity, that which would end your continued people! There is no so-called "human race" and nor would we want such a thing! For such a thing would tend to erase our uniqueness, our beauty, our own race itself precisely as mere *belief* in that myth of a "human race" is doing today! The "human race" myth breaks down the actual races, their individual unique existences, and is that not in fact the intent of the myth? For the myth of the "human race" seeks to bring the actual races together whereas they must be apart if they wish to continue to live and be who they really are.

How true it is that shortsightedness has been the bane of our history, and so has compassion at our own expense! We have been furthermore enamored by silly slogans and irrationalities paraded as truths, duped by a verbiage, and fleeced by foolish-

143

ness. Know that almost everything on your boob tube represents a fantasy world, that what is *said* to be important is *not* important, that the politics of today are devoid of any worth, and that all of the energies of the present society are misplaced! The issue is not "wars" on terrorism or drugs, "the future of the country," deficits or debts, whether the planet is getting warmer or not, or any number of other topics incessantly discussed like the turning of a merry-go-round, but whether a race, our race, will live! Precisely the issue that is *not* discussed on the boob tube! How quaint that all "debates" stay clear of this issue, instead distracting us from *the* issue that makes all else pale! How quaint that all "debates" keep us in a line heading for slaughter!

The politicians talk about "existential threats" to the United States, for example, and yet when it comes to true existence, our *racial* existence, no words are thought about let alone spoken! How odd it is indeed that people can care about supposed "existential threats" to a State, to a society, or even to a world for that matter without any regard or thought being paid to the existential threats to the race which forms them! What State though can matter more than a race? What society though can matter more than a race? What world can even be conceived of having an importance aside from the races that inhabit it? Race is the wheel, the wheels, of every vehicle, there being no movement without it. Sooner would we lovers of our White Race, of our White culture, of our White identity, want every State, society, or world consigned to the flames before our race is itself consigned to dust! For we know that every facet of States, societies, and of the world can only have significance in regard to how they affect *us*, how they affect *our* existence, and that which *we* value! Thus if terrorism is bad, it is bad for men, *White* men. If drugs are bad, they are bad for men, *White* men. If we are concerned about the future of the country, it is because men are in it, *White* men. If there is high unemployment, it is obviously men who are out of work, *White* men. If the government is massively in debt, what matters is how that might hurt men, *White* men. If the planet is really getting warmer, we are concerned about the effects on men, *White* men. Thus every topic of concern for people is inseparable from the fact that people are involved and the fact that people are involved is inseparable from the fact that *White* people are involved! Yes, we don't want our White people out of work. Yes, we don't want our White people maimed or murdered by terrorists. Yes, we don't want our White people destroying their minds through drug use. Yes, we don't want White people in any country to have no future regardless of whether the countries themselves have a future. Yes, we don't want White people to be at the whim, caprice, or mercy of any other people. To specifically ignore or shun White people *as a people* from such concerns would thus be to distract us from the root of why such concerns matter! And, more importantly, without a live White Race, what matters such concerns? Without a White Race remaining in existence, the employment, health, and lives of White people are the concern only of forgotten dreams, undreamt by anyone still alive. To take race out of the equation then is, as always, to render the equation worthless. We value the world by our participation in it; to sacrifice our participation in it, our *existence* in it, is to sacrifice its value, for *us*.

The true "existential threat" is easy to explain: we White people are outnumbered 14 to 1 (by races who have been wrongly taught that we have "oppressed" them), we are shrinking in population still, and sizeable numbers of our people are mongrelizing with the other races as well. Now *there* is an "existential threat" worth talking about! We are disappearing from this earth and the process will only be hastened by the presence of the non-whites amongst us. The rate of our mongrelization will increase with that presence and who is to say that as our numbers become fewer and fewer, we will not face all-out murder at their hands as a consequence? After all, if it is true that we "held everybody else down" as they claim, why should they not want revenge at some point in the future when we no longer have the means nor the numbers to successfully defend ourselves? That is what you call looking ahead, foresight, which every race must have if it is to be secure in its existence. No less must we have it if we are to be secure in ours. It is foolish to leave the future of our race in the good graces of the other races, is it not?

The world abounds with ideas but what idea can possibly be more important than the physical world that precedes them all, the physicality of race that precedes all ideas? A million thoughts may transpire between our ears but they can never trump the reality of our blood! No idea, no matter how seemingly grand, how lofty, how novel can ever be allowed to counter the racial law of life! That is the mistake that we have indeed made as a race, my Brothers and Sisters, the thought that our intellectualisms can somehow supersede the reality of our racial existence or that they should! This White man here calls himself a Republican; that White man there calls himself a Democrat. Another White man calls himself a Socialist; another White man calls himself a Nationalist; another a Conservative, another still a Social Democrat, and on and on while all the while, all of them have forgotten, have ignored, have even divested themselves of what they have in common: that they are all White! That is the common ground that precedes all claims to various political perspectives. This is the common ground that literally stares us in the face! Long enough have we factionalized ourselves, fractionalized ourselves, divided ourselves between ideas formed in our heads when all along our race and only our race was the proper yardstick! This political philosophy has appealed to this man, that to another, and another to another still when all along those political philosophies come and go like the wind while the race that formed them remains! Make whatever political philosophies that exist now or in the future serve our *race*, not the other way around, my Brothers and Sisters! Neither the symbol of an elephant nor the symbol of a jackass can hold a candle to the flesh and blood White man, woman, and child! How could we ever have been so foolish to think that they could? The bond of blood is the mighty tidal wave that sweeps the factions before it; no longer do we cancel each other out! No longer are there "aisles" separating White people, rather one people filling one hall! And nor do the colors of our flags, the colors of our political logos, or the colors of anything else somehow supersede the color of our skin! No economic theory, no social values, no large or small government espousal, no borders, no class or clique can supersede the race that preceded them all! What passions, what energies, what angst have been expended upon the mere momentary trappings of a race while all along the foundation of every dwelling remained the same: the race itself. How we Racial Loyalists almost feel like weeping when we witness our people wringing their hands agonizing over abstractions and distractions concerning mere contrivances of ideology while the root of their life, their race, goes to pot, forfeiting its existence, acquiescing in its genocide. Men are willing to duke it out over stupid political parties but are unwilling to clasp hands as White Brothers and Sisters? Egad the idiocy of our time that must be destroyed! Smash the foolishness of factionalism. Erase the delusion of dividedness. Tear down the false idols, ushering forth their twilight. The moment a White man does *not* speak with his race in mind, he is in error; the moment that a politics is uttered that *isn't* based upon White identity, White love, White preservation, and White advancement, substance is being sacrificed for surface and truth is being sacrificed for trinkets.

The world has always swirled with ideas, ideas about religion, ideas about politics, ideas abut philosophy, ideas about social customs, ideas that are very important to the people at the time only to disappear in short order while the race that evoked the ideas remains. Thus it is the race that is more important than the ideas, not the ideas that are more important than the race! While ideas have come and gone throughout history, your race has not, my Brothers and Sisters! It remains alive for you today to fight for while on the other hand, the ideas that dazzled your ancestors have ceased to exist! How our people have been caught up in their particular ideas while ignoring their race which transcends all ideas! Indeed, how our people have been charmed by ideas that are hostile to their racial survival! For while races *should* be permanent upon this earth, excepting due to natural disasters or environmental changes that cannot be helped, if the ideas they embrace are bad enough, their embrace by the people *can* destroy the races foolish enough to embrace them! This is what we have going on today, of course. We have ideas that are embraced that not only disregard our survival but positively discourage it such as "anti-racism," "the equality of man," and non-white immigration into our countries, societies, and neighborhoods. The minds of the people are devoted to such ideas and the White Race as a race can go to hell as far as they are concerned. Thoughts that have come—and will certainly go, sooner or later—have taken total precedence over the race that both preceded them and will succeed them too provided that the thoughts don't destroy us first. It is time to reverse this bizarre situation whereby an idea, *any* idea, can be allowed to militate against our racial survival. It is time to reverse the situation by which the mere *thoughts* of a race are deemed more important than the race itself! In a sense, this is the crux of the issue for the future: should our race serve the raw *ideas* that come willy-nilly into our heads, or should whatever ideas that exist serve our flesh and blood, body and soul, cultural and genetic *race*? Indeed, it goes even further than that: should our race also serve governments, societies, fads or fashions, various customs, etc. (which are also *ideas*) or should governments, societies, and everything else serve our *race*?

Dare I say that the answer to these questions is quite plain, my Brothers and Sisters? What mere idea could ever be more important than our race; how could we ever allow any mere thought to *harm* our race? Should we not devote ourselves to the preservation of that which, absent environmental or natural disaster, will be permanent rather than to notions created by men that inevitably, sooner or later, leave the world stage? Should not our race be the master in our hearts rather than the servant? One of them *has* to be master and one of them *has* to be the servant because race and ideas is all there is: either our race will in fact serve our ideas or our ideas will serve our *race*; either ideas will direct the physicality or the physicality will direct the ideas as it should be! Our race has adhered to countless religions, forms of governments, customs, philosophies, and so forth throughout its history. We have worshipped Zeus, Odin, Jesus, and others; loved monarchy, aristocracy, democracy, even anarchy; have treated foreigners as our house guests and as our foes; have drank beer in one place and wine in another; and have embraced the philosophies of philosophers as different as Aristotle and St. Augustine and Rousseau and Nietzsche. While every generation likes to think that its own ideas and attitudes are "modern" and somehow therefore better than those of the previous generations, and that their ideas and attitudes will somehow continue to exist and be embraced in all likelihood in perpetuity, what we know from history instead is that *no* ideas and attitudes, customs and the like are permanent. Indeed, *the only thing that has continued to exist is the race that came up with them.* "Democracy" is all the rage today for example but it was all the rage in 5th century BC Athens too until the people there threw it out. The Czar of Russia was ousted in 1917 but there is today talk in some circles of putting one back on the throne. States have come and gone throughout history notwithstanding the devotion of their citizens; men fought and died for Livonia, the Holy Roman Empire, Babylonia, Khazaria, Assyria, and many others but do these States survive today? Europe was ruled by Christendom for nearly a thousand years but today Christianity there is at best an influence upon the individual inhabitants and not so much at that. True, the advent of the technological age has tended to make ideas more universal but there is no reason to believe that such ideas will be any more permanent now than they were in the past. There may be a "universal love for freedom," for example, but that love is within a Muslim context in the Middle East, a secular ostensibly Christian context in Europe, a Hindu, Buddhist, and atheist context in Asia, and a religiously potpourri context in America and thus "freedom" means different things accordingly. What is considered acceptable to religious believers has changed throughout the centuries as well, Christianity being the most obvious example. If ideas could be so different at different times among different peoples and among different races, and could come and go and sometimes come back again at that, ideas cannot be what is most important.

Instead, what is most important is the *race* which exists independently of any ideas, the *race* that remains long after this or that idea has become passé, the *race* that churns out the ideas in the first place, in our case the White *race* since we are indeed White. Gone must be the subservience of an unending race to unenduring ideas. Preference must be given to the race over any ideas!

And yet with us, my Racial Loyalist Brothers and Sisters, we have a unique situation, for we too have an idea which we love but it happens to *be* our race! Thus unlike with every other idea in history, *our* idea is *not* something that comes and goes but rather remains as our race remains. *Our* idea is thus not artificial and transitory but rather natural and enduring; it is an idea not based on abstractions, desires, or whims but rather is based upon the physical world itself! Our thinking coincides with our blood. Our values revolve *around* our blood. First comes our race and then comes our thinking, not the reverse! First comes our race and then comes our morals, not the reverse! Our blood came before any thinking in time and so we say that our thinking must be dependent upon that blood. Our blood continues *after* any particular thinking and so we say that our thinking must likewise be dependent upon that blood. Our blood, our race is the stream itself while ideas are the mere temporary waves. With us though, with we Racial Loyalists, our ideas and our blood become one! The idea of White identity, White loyalty, and White love is based upon the natural, preceding existence of White people in this world; we exist and so these sentiments exist. We existed before there were any religions, any States, any governments, any philosophies, and on and on and so these things should serve *us* and our *continued* existence. Man can devise much and he is capable of devising both wonderful and horrible things, but *nothing he devises can be more important than him himself*. This is the idea, the noble idea that we hold dear, that Man must finally come first in the hearts and minds of men, that our race must come first in the hearts and minds of our race!

What a change this is from the way things have been! White

people have been quarreling with one another—and worse—for untold thousands of years over religious ideas, political ideas, social ideas, moral and ethical ideas, and every other idea that they have been capable of merely conjuring up in their heads, while sadly ignoring and discounting the raw fact that *unites* all White men: that we are all White! All along the love of our race should have united us but we instead cast our minds into a net of abstractions and distractions, looking beyond ourselves when *ourselves* should have been our everything! Our race is the sun around which all planets (ideas) should rightly revolve. Our race is the yardstick by which all should be measured. We White lovers say no more to our race being subordinate to its own creations, the ideas that we favor and discard as time, and our race, goes on. We who create say let no more priority be given to our various creations but rather let it be given to us creators! If every idea about everything were to somehow leave our minds at this instant, our race would remain. Thus our race comes first, last, and always. Race is what not only unites us regardless of any ideas that swirl about the world but the time has finally come to subordinate all ideas, consciously and avowedly, to the benefit of the race. (This of course goes for *ideals* as well!) Does this particular idea benefit White people? If it does, it is a good idea to support and extol. If it doesn't, it is a bad idea to disclaim and discard. This is the revolution that we preach, my Brothers and Sisters! It is not good enough to ask, for example, whether multiracialism might be good for "people"; the question for us is whether it is good for *White* people. Does it, in other words, support our continued cultural, genetic, and biological existence as a race? It is not good enough, as another example, to ask whether "free trade" might be good for "people"; the question for us as White people, naturally enough, is whether it is good for *White* people. Does it support our continued cultural, genetic, and biological existence as a race? At times we may be able to disagree as to the answer to that question but the question must always be asked or assumed at the forefront of our minds. Does this social order, this political order, this philosophy, this way of looking at the world in general support our continued cultural, genetic, and biological existence as a race? How could we ever have failed, or can we ever again fail, to ask that question? Our race literally stares back at us in the mirror, our blood courses in our veins, the world is full of races of every description of every animal, insect, fish, amphibian, and so forth that devote themselves entirely to their own respective races, and yet we, the most gifted of all, haven't focused on what benefits *our* race, our unique race, out of the multitudes? Let your thinking now be directed by that. Let your values now be formed by that. Let your ideals rest upon your own physical reality. Secure a place for your race in the sun. Race before all ideas, not ideas before the race! Race before all governments (ideas), not governments (ideas) before the race! And on and on no matter how unsettling to the status quo, to others, and to ourselves that may be! The race remains when these things have withered away. Only the racial idea itself, bound up with the enduring race, endures with it likewise, the only idea based upon the only eternal, natural physicality in this world. To have an idea based upon something concrete for a change, how refreshing! To have an idea independent of personality-type, independent of social circumstances, independent of age and the age in question; to have an idea that is the same for every generation and that provides common, unassailable purpose; to have a sun that draws all of our gazes and bestows all of our warmth—what joy it is that we may no longer be prisoners of our own minds, that we may instead look upon our racial being and say that *this* is our meaning, *this* is our cause, *this* is our yearning: ourselves! Our being that makes all else subsidiary, life which is the master! Our race the compass, the yardstick, the barometer for the world around us. Never again lost will we be; never again will we be like ships passing in the night, the world a shadowed, inexplicable mystery.

My Brothers and Sisters, do not ever allow the actions of others in the past to be laid at your doorstep; their history is not your story, their errors are not your fruit. You need not explain or justify anything in the past for you had no part in it. No doubt the haters of White life, of a White Race extant, assertive, and proud of itself would like you to fall into that trap, the trap of defense where no defense is necessary! They would like to associate you with causes and movements and actions that they have thoroughly propagandized the people into disdaining so that the people will disdain you as well! Indeed, they want you to step upon a muddy path even if they themselves happen to be responsible for the mud! They wish to replace your credit with discredit, your love with hate, your foresight with nostalgia. They wish to show that the case is closed with you before it has even begun! They wish to mire you in the struggles of the past rather than defer to your clear path of now, today, and tomorrow. Resist their invitations. You are not responsible for anything that occurred before you were born and so you need not defend it. You owned no slave, denied no one his so-called "civil rights," persecuted no one, and no war was your doing! Yes the errors of the past can be explored but an explanation is not a subscription. They think they know who you are because they have placed you in a category of their own creation. They have applied labels to you that do not fit, ascribed motivations to you that are not real, and have felt smug while doing it! How they would love for their mythologies to be validated through your playing their game, accepting their characterizations, defending their alleged villainies, and refighting their favored controversies for which verdicts have supposedly already been rendered! Deny them this, my Brothers and Sisters; do not follow their script! Instead turn the tables on their machinations! It is *they* who are the "haters," not you. It is *they* who are the enemies of freedom, not you. It is *they* who wish to destroy while you wish to preserve. It is *they* who are out for chaos. It is *they* who are the assailants of Man, of Nature, of Life! It is *they* who are the disrupters of peace, harmony, and order. It is *they* who have not thought through their prescriptions, they who would despoil tomorrow for today! It is *they* who wish to lower Man while you wish to raise him. In sum, their so-called "civil rights workers" are simply black and brown racists, their drive for so-called "equality" is simply a cloak for anti-White hostility, and their espousal of misnamed "diversity" amounts to an advocacy of genocide!

Let them be asked why they are so keen about the erasure of the White Race upon the face of this earth, and if they deny that they are in fact so keen, ask them why is it then that they oppose the creation of policies that would prevent that from occurring, such as all-White neighborhoods, all-White societies, and all-White countries and why they even deny that White people have a valuable, unique existence at all! The answer that such would be "racist" is no answer because of course it is "racist" since we are dealing with a race! And likewise the moment a black man, brown man, or yellow man cares about the welfare of *his* race, *he* is racist and is engaging in racism too! It is no answer for him to call his racism something else! It doesn't matter whether the racism is dressed up as "civil rights" or anything else! It doesn't matter whether it is defensive or offensive, pretentious or unpretentious, with the sense of a need or a want, with the sense of an entitlement or a mere yearning, with a reliance on supposed law or supposed moral authority, or any number of other trappings! Racism it is, whether it be likeable or dislikeable in the particular case at hand, as it is the assertion, the recognition, of a race! We lovers of White identity, of White genes, of White solidarity have no more need to defend our "racism" than do the black and brown racists their own racism in their (actually non-existent) campaign for so-called equal rights! They want alleged equal rights for a *race* and thus are practitioners of racism. Their racism may be positive for *them* but so is our racism for *us*. Their racism may have the effect of advancing *them* but so does our racism have the effect of advancing *us*. Banish from your mind that a racism for "equality" is somehow better, more moral, more just than a racism for genetic, cultural, and biological *survival*! It isn't and can never be. They want the same so-called "rights" as us? Who cares? We want to live! They demand "equality" in society? We want a different society than the present one altogether! They have no right to determine *our* moral yardstick and we do not determine *theirs*. They have no right to expect that while they progress as black, brown, and yellow races that *we* must be content with *regress* as a White Race! Enough of such idiocy now and forevermore!

My Brothers and Sisters, "progress" is and always has been a subjective word. It does not and cannot reflect the same estimation of the present state of affairs for everyone and indeed, the way those opposed to an extant, proud, assertive White Race would have it, "progress," when it comes to race, is *only* that which benefits every other race and *not* the White! How quaint! We hear again and again what "progress" we have made in America on race, for example, but never, for even one instant, is it said that *White* people, as a race, have benefitted by the supposed "progress." Instead it is simply assumed that they must have since the *other* races have. Let us therefore cease being befuddled by their use of the word "progress." Their use of the word does not apply to us! Their "progress" is in fact our regress. Their "civil rights" are our *civil wrongs*. Their advancement has been our *decline*. The "progress" of one group is the regress of another but they would rather that you not know that lest *their* progress— at your expense—come to a halt through your awakening! Instead, so long as you think that "progress" automatically means whatever in reality benefits races *other* than your own, you will not lift a finger to halt the *regress* of your own people and that's what they want! Indeed, they have caused you to forget that White people are even *capable* of benefitting by any policy that doesn't at the same time benefit the other races! You have been told over and over what "progress" we've made concerning race, "how far we've come" and the like, as a means of destroying your own thought processes for your own people! Such is the trickery of the terminology of those who seek your dispossession: get White people to accept the definitions of their own value judgments, value judgments that are in fact hostile to our continued existence as a people! They want the advancement of the *non-white* races so they use the word "progress" so often, in relation to that, that White people become convinced that that is indeed progress, for *White* people. They want what White people have so they call that "civil rights," implying of course that they have a "right" to it. They don't like all-White neighborhoods, communities, or countries so they introduce the charming word "diversity" in order to break them up. They want White people to acquiesce in their dispossession so they laud the virtues of "tolerance." (What they really mean is *surrender!*) They espouse a love of "multiculturalism" because everyone has a positive regard for culture, right? They deplore as "hatred" *whatever resists them.* No one can deny them their great talent in the manipulation of words! Do not accede to such manipulations. Do not refer to their alleged "civil rights movement" that does not actually exist. Do not allow them to get away with calling our dispossession as a people "progress." Do not allow them to speak well of "diversity" when they are actually committed to the *destruction* of diversity in men. Do not accept that appreciation of "tolerance" means that you can't want a secure future for your own kind. Do not accept the label of "white supremacist" when you are and always have been opposed to White people reigning supreme over the other races in any form or fashion; wanting White people to have a future is no more "white supremacy" than is wanting the same for black people "black supremacy" and the like! And have enough love in your hearts that you can withstand their smears of "hatred"! Their manipulation of words is now finally countered, and if the counter can one day be successful amongst the hundreds of millions of our people, the manipulation of their minds will also come to an end! It is no easy task but it must be done. The manipulation of words happily grows stale, the edifice based upon it begins to totter! A tall but dilapidated shack can indeed be pushed down with effort, energy, and will! A new progress is on the way! A real progress because as a race, our White people advances! Benefit to another race is finally talked about: ours! May the values that have been hurting us finally be overthrown!

To achieve that though, my Brothers and Sisters, you must be better than the lies you despise. You must be stronger than what you deride as weakness. You must be superior to that which is claimed to be "equal." If you wish to change the present world, you must show that you are better than it. It is not enough to have an opinion; you must show not only that the opinion is right but that you yourselves are great! It is not enough to reject the present order; you must instead show your people that *excellent* men reject it! The morass of mediocrity can be defeated by no other course; the status quo has held the day for too long, its mass too dense, its weight too heavy. It will take skill, wisdom, and talent to move a passed out, drunken elephant! You must become better than you can readily contemplate. Frivolities must be minimal for you. That which bedazzles the masses you must give barely a glance. If you have vices, you must earn them through your self-improvement in other respects! Minimize your vices then and maximize your virtues! To believe in your blood, your family, your kind, your race is not enough; you must also learn how to speak, how to write, how to comport yourselves, and hence how to persuade! Where others have told themselves that they have done enough, you must tell yourself that there is still more to do. Where others feel a sense of contentedness, you must feel a gnawing sense that there is more for you to strive. You must defy the delusions of those who would like to think that you are of low personal character, of low worth, and of base motives; the dissipation of such delusions will lead to the dissipation of their other delusions as well! Yes you wish to rain upon their present parade but only as a prelude to a rainbow-filled sky! Yes you are for your White Race in all things and at all times but that is cause for commendation, not alarm!

To improve the self precedes the improvement of anything else. Look at time as not something to "pass" but rather as an opportunity by which to *gain*! In mind, body, and spirit you must become someone whom others will admire and wish to emulate; then they will have a great regard and appreciation for the cause that you yourself regard and appreciate. How easy it is to deride a cause when its proponent seems to be so lacking; how much more difficult it is to do when its proponent is a quality man! That then is the task before you: be and become a quality man! Needless to say, not an *e*-quality man but rather a *quality* man! May I motivate you, the cause of White Life motivate you, and may you motivate yourself. When those who are not yet with us expect you to spew, you must instead articulate. When they expect you to abuse, you must disabuse. When they expect you to be timid, you must be bold. When they expect you to be ignorant, you must lead them to conclude that they themselves have been in ignorance. When they expect you to be close-minded, you must show that it is actually they who have had their minds in boxes, indeed in chains! You are not the ones who froth at the mouth; you are not the ones who gnash their teeth late at night! Such is the silliness of those who have not known any better, who have justified their own ignorance with thoughts of mania on your part!

Where they expect you to be barely literate, you must show that you indeed know how to read and well; indeed, you realize it is not the quantity but the *quality* that counts. The books that you read may never grace any best seller lists but then again the greatest, most important books never have! You realize that there is a great difference between reading much and being well-read; many a tree has lost its life for the printing of a particular book but too bad the tree's life had greater value much of the time! May you always be ready to match your quality with their quantity; your knowledge with their verbiage; your exploration with their mere assumption. When they expect you to have no conscience, you must show them your conscientiousness. When they expect you to be rabid you must hold up a mirror to reveal to them their own rabidity!

Do your best to have a command of the language you speak, being able to use the ideal word for every thought or emotion you wish to convey, for the broad grasp of language will give you a power! You will learn which word to use at which time as the best means of persuasion. You will not do your thinking only as you speak but will have done your thinking long before the particular words have ever left your mouth; your thinking for your White Race, your White identity, your White family which is the backdrop for everything you think, say, and do!

My Brothers and Sisters, you have now come far in your liberation from mental slavery. You no longer are apologetic for being White, no longer believe yourself to be in debt to the other races due to imaginary wrongs supposedly suffered at your race's hands, and no longer take the words of manipulation directed at your people at face value; indeed, you now realize that you are indeed a people whose proper devotion belongs to itself! A people with its own culture, its own uniqueness, its own freedom to pursue its eternal life on this earth, and likewise its own best interests in every other respect. You have now achieved racial consciousness and the chains that enslaved your mind have been broken! You are no longer beholden to any society and the artificial values that it may deign to impose but realize instead that any and all societies where your people live are more rightly beholden to *you*, your people, your race, your blood, your kind! A politician may likewise claim that you have a duty to think and do such and such as a citizen but you know that your duty is instead as a Brother and Sister of your race. Neither society nor citizenship can ever mean more than your family, your Racial Family! A social security card or a driver's license does not mean more than your blood! There can be no competition between an external identity imposed upon you and the identity that you bear each and every day of your life from birth to death: the blood of your family and your extended family, your race. Languages can be learned, citizenships can be changed, wealth can be gained or lost, but your race remains constant, constantly yours and you constantly its. The television is not your true identity. The politics of the time are not your true identity. The money in your pocket is not your true identity. Your employment is not your true identity. Lines on a map do not compose your true identity. Your religion is not your true identity. Of course you value some or all of these things but they are more accurately facets of your daily living and life, not your true *identity*. Television may well provide you with some knowledge and entertainment on occasion. The current politics may well be of interest to you or in fact amuse you. Money improves your standard of living. Excelling at your employment may well provide you with a sense of accomplishment and should. Religion may well provide you with a personal sense of salvation, of joy, and of hope. Your identity though is that which you were *born* with and that which you will die with: your race. Resolve to yourself that you will let no mere idea trump it, including your own! Let there be the flowering of thought but not at the expense of the garden. Let there be the flowering of personalities but not at the expense of the race itself.

To win our race to the Racial Idea is no small task but it must be done if our race is to continue to exist. You must lift your voices, disdaining silence. You must reply with the contrary to every crooked word. You must organize and demonstrate en masse against the current order, challenging all of its precepts and its inevitable result should it not be changed: the annihilation of your race. A raceless society, a "colorblind" society, cannot preserve our race nor of course can a society that is racial for the *non*-whites but *anti*-racial for the Whites which is what we have in America, though not necessarily all other places, today. The White Race is not preserved when its numbers are on the decline and that of the other races are on the vast incline. The White Race is not preserved when a sizeable percentage of it interbreeds with the other races. The White Race is not preserved when its youth, and all generations of it in fact, ape the other races, their cultures, their habits, and even their mindsets. The White Race is not preserved when most people have been hoodwinked into thinking that its preservation doesn't even matter and that a person must be bad for thinking that it does. The White Race is not preserved when its habitat is overrun and repopulated by the other races. The White Race is not preserved when some of its most "elite" members spend their entire lives advancing the welfare of the other races and disregarding totally the welfare of their own race. No, the problem is not in our own minds; the problem is real: the current order is anti-White preservation and thus must be replaced. Only men (and women of course) can do the replacing: you. It starts with understanding, it ends with victory: your victory. You are the means and you are the end. We either desire our preservation or we don't for there is no in-between. And if we indeed desire our preservation, we must necessarily take those steps which achieve that preservation! It is as simple as that. Gone must be the idea that life is about willy-nilly selfishness or a *non*-racial altruism! Rather, the meaning of life is the preservation of our race, blood, kind! This is your altruism, your preservation of self!

Freely you now disdain being raceless; freely you now speak your race as well as wear it proudly! Freely you now proclaim your allegiance to your race in any and all things; freely you announce that your citizenship is one of blood! And what does citizenship require, my Brothers and Sisters? A State!

Chapter Three
Towards the Racial State

We have seen the city-state and we have seen the empire; we have seen the nation-state, the multi-racial state, and we have also seen the (now) multi-racial union of states referred to as the United States of America. Perhaps we have seen other forms of States as well, but one thing seems to be certain: we have never seen the *Racial* State, the State that is not only composed of one race but which is also devoted exclusively to that one race. *It is now time that we see the formation of such a State.* This may turn out to be the hardest portion of my words to accept for some and yet it follows ineluctably from all of the preceding. It may be the hardest portion to accept because we have grown so accustomed to the States as they currently exist and have attached great sentiment to them as well. And yet, as discussed earlier, States have come and gone throughout history; when the then currently existing States did not satisfy the desires or needs of the people in question, the people formed new States that did. This is, in fact, the fundamental premise of the Declaration of Independence of the United States of America, a declaration by States that did not exist previously but which were now declared to exist because the previous, possessor State (Great Britain) was allegedly destructive to the "life, liberty, and pursuit of happiness" of the people which is the purpose for which States are formed, according to the authors. Thus it cannot be revolutionary in itself merely to assert now that which the declarants of independence for the United States already declared more than 235 years ago: that when people are dissatisfied with their present States (political entities with borders), they are entitled to create new ones. There is nothing revolutionary about that at all as it is the founding premise of our very own current United States of America.

What *is* though revolutionary is that we lovers of White life now want a *Racial* State. Yes, we want a State that is composed exclusively of our race, our White Race, and yes, unlike all States apparently of the past, we want the State to be *devoted overtly and exclusively to that race*. While *having* States of exclusively one race was, of course, nothing unusual in the past since races instinctively desire to live apart from one another and have done so throughout history, in this day and age of "multiracialism" it *is* exceptional to reject the latter insane ideology and to want a *homogeneous* State instead yet again and furthermore one that is also devoted *exclusively* to that race as a matter of *policy*. This combination makes us different all right, different from today and different from yesterday. And yet, the basic principle declared by the signers of the Declaration of Independence remains the same: States are the *choice* of the people and that people thus has the option to form new States when the old ones become destructive to their lives, their liberty, and their pursuit of happiness, those terms of course being defined by the people in question. It is not good enough for the governments of the (current) States to say, in other words, that the lives, liberty, and pursuit of happiness of the people are being preserved just fine if the people do not themselves happen to agree. Rather, it is up to the people themselves to decide if those conditions have in fact been met and to form new governments if not. This principle is as American, indeed as freedom loving, as it gets even if it is the case that the politicians in charge of the current States certainly do not want us to think of it. *Of course* they would like the people to think that all States are a "done" deal, both for sentimental reasons and because they enjoy their own power, and yet, all the while, the fact of the matter is that new States continue to form! Who had ever heard of the States of South Sudan, East Timor, Moldova, and Kosovo until recently, for example? Every line on a map was someplace else at one time. Let us accept that fact and accept the principle that people continue to have the option to form new States as both declared—and acted out—by our forefathers. And for those of us who are indeed Americans, that principle did not somehow die at our *birth*, the birth of the United States of America, as someone could be tempted to say! No indeed, it would make little sense for us, in the name of Americanism, to deny the very premise of the United States of America. Instead, the very premise upon which our American States were founded *negates any claim that the premise does not still exist* and one cannot sensibly celebrate the independence of those States every July 4th *and yet be hostile to the very premise of that independence*.

So, let us accept the principle that people, our White people specifically, have the option to form new political entities with borders, States, if we so choose and that is the case even if the current States are changed or cease to exist in the process. The latter may be an unsettling notion on its face but again, it is the founding premise of the United States of America as corroborated by a reading of their Declaration of Independence. Great Britain obviously changed when it lost its American colonies (now States) but that is the way it goes. So have other States changed or even ceased to exist throughout history due to the formation of new ones. The very founders of the United States of America would no doubt agree with the proposition that those States, quite simply, are not as important as the people themselves: their lives, their liberty, and their pursuit of happiness as they put it. Otherwise they would not have formed the United States in the first place.

The matter of States, countries, and nations has been confused for a long time and it is important that that confusion be unraveled at the outset so that my words may be properly and totally understood. Simply put, States are political entities with borders, as indicated earlier; countries are *geographical* entities; and nations are *ethnic* entities. That is what I mean when I use these terms. I use these terms in their historical, traditional, and indeed *accurate* manner rather than confusingly mixing them together as almost always happens today. For example, there is no "nation" called the United States of America because the United States of America are *political* entities (States) and America itself is a *geographical* entity. As another example, think about the term "nation-state": it is the nation (the ethnic group) that resides in the *State*, not the reverse! In other words, the reality is that nations reside in *States*, not that States are part of a "nation." Otherwise, the historic term "nation-state" would make no sense, its meaning being that a State is composed of a particular ethnic group, a nation. The Jewish *nation*, for example, has existed for thousands of years but the Israeli *State* was only founded in 1948. By the same token, the German nation has also existed for thousands of years but the Federal Republic of Germany, composed of various States, was likewise founded after the Second World War. As another obvious example, there are numerous American Indian nations *within* the United States, the status of these particular nations being recognized by federal law. Other examples could be cited without limit but what is essential is to simply remember that States are *political* entities (with borders), countries are *lands*, and nations are *peoples*. The creation of new *States* notably has no impact upon the number of *nations* that exist and indeed, to cite the Germans again, the German *nation* exists in Austria, Switzerland, Liechtenstein, the various *States* composing today's German Republic, and elsewhere. In other words, since a nation is a *people*, a nation can transcend States just as a *race* can transcend States and of course do; just as the German nation exists in sever-al States, the larger White Race exists in several, indeed multiple States. Austrians are part of the German *nation* but reside in the Austrian *State*. Poland is a State where the majority of the Polish *nation* resides but a sizeable part of the Polish nation also resides in the United *States*. Englishmen are part of the English *nation* but reside in the United Kingdom of Great Britain and Northern Ireland, a kingdom of *States*.

These examples are probably more than necessary but the more that State, country, and nation are kept distinct as to their meaning, the greater the understanding and, in regards to the White Racial State which we who love White Life desire, the greater will be the acceptance of same. We hence want a Racial State but that does not mean that we seek to hurt any *nation*, for instance, and nor does it mean that we do not love our *country*. On the contrary, we love our country very much: we love the mountains, we love the forests, we love the plains, and thus we love *the land*. We may also very well love much of what goes on in that land. That though does not mean that we have to love, or should love, the current political arrangement by which that land is ruled. By means of analogy, both the Northerner and the Southerner during the horrible 1861-1865 War Between the States were Americans, loved America, and thus were *patriots* but they simply were not in accord as to the *political* arrangement of the *States*; both were loyal to the *country* but did not agree as to the proper *political* situation by which to live. The Southern States wanted to be part of a new union of States called a confederacy but the Northern States refused to let them go. It is simply wrong to claim, as occurred then and occurs now due to confusion as to what the various terms actually mean, that somehow the Southern States ceased to be part of *America* when they left the United States because, once again, a country is independent of any States that happen to be formed on it. Thus we had United States of America and Confederate States of America, both being of course *of* America. America was the *land*, not a "nation" and nor a State. (Furthermore, of course, the United States today, since they are *States* rather than a singular "State," are *plural*, not singular.) Again, States are simply political entities with borders; the changing of those borders does not change the country nor of course the nation or nations (the peoples) that live there. All of these terms mean something different from one another—States, countries, nations, and even society and environment—and it behooves us to finally realize that. Mixing them all together, as has been done, has destroyed clarity as well as set people at odds with one another needlessly. When the meanings of words are confused, everyone loses.

There thus have been States of different types throughout history and new States come into being on a routine basis. Because States are political entities, this is not really surprising as the political beliefs of peoples are in constant flux, these political beliefs changing based upon changes in society, outside pressures, tyrannical rule, and so forth. Sometimes States are formed also by virtue of the breakup of empires; the States that formed as a result of the breakup of the Ottoman Empire in 1919 are an obvious example of this. One thing seems to be quite evident: the number of States tends to always be on the *increase* rather than on the decrease. We do not hear much about existing States merging together but we *do* hear about existing States breaking apart. There used to be a State called "Czechoslovakia," for instance, but now there are two separate States, the Czech State and the Slovak State. Bangladesh used to be part of Pakistan but is now its own State. East Timor used to be part of Indonesia but is now its own State. The end of the British and French empires in Africa resulted in the creation of dozens of new States. There are, in fact, more than twice as many States in the world now as there were a mere hundred years ago. Thus despite concerns about one world government, there are actually more *governments* than ever, within their respective States. New States are formed, new flags are created for those States, and these States quickly become "recognized members of the world community" as they say. Another place setting has to be made in the (misnamed) United "Nations" General Assembly. Today the Palestinians are campaigning for such recognition of the State of Palestine to exist alongside the current State of Israel, for example, and if it hadn't been for American veto power at the UN and Jewish power around the world, they undoubtedly would have obtained that State a long time ago.

Nobody ever seems to ask whether a particular people *deserves* a State; rather, as with the Founding Fathers of the United States, that is simply assumed: if that people decide that they want a new State, then we share in their aspiration. There may be complications—and those complications need to be worked out—but there is no denying that people our *sympathy*. Thus college students in America hold signs reading "Free Tibet" and the like. Thus even military aid is sometimes given as occurred, for example, when the United States supported the new Panamanian State in its early 20th century severance from Colombia or the new Cuban State in its late 19th century severance from Spain. The creation of new States may not *always* be supported where it is not clear that the bulk of the people really want the new State but where that *is* clear, support for the creation of such new

States is indeed customary. No existing State is thus set in stone. This includes *unions* of States as well, such as that of the United States of America; have we not seen many new States join that union over time? We started with thirteen, after all, and now we have fifty. The fact that those States joined a *union* of States rather than choosing to exist separately, as do other States in the world, is of no consequence. They are States all the same, being merely part of a union of them called the United States of America. Each one of the United States of America has its own constitution, its own borders, and its own flag. They are States just the same as the other States throughout the world, only that by joining the federal union of States, they have willingly ceded some of their power to the government of that union, the federal government, as specified by the charter of that federal government, the Constitution of the United States.

All in all, when we consider the matter rationally, historically, and accurately, we must come to the conclusion that States have received far more adoration than they are due. They are, to say it for maybe the last time, merely *political entities*. They are of a finite duration while, on the other hand, the races or nations that inhabit them, and the land itself, have an *infinite* duration. In other words, while the States come and go, the peoples and the land remain. It stands to reason therefore that the people, the race in our case, must, once again, *come before any State* and not the reverse. Quite plainly and directly let it be said that the destruction of our White Race would be a far, far worse calamity than the dissolution of the United States or of any *other* State for that matter. This is so, yet again, because States are finite *political entities*. Finite political entities cannot possibly matter more than our race itself. As our American Founding Fathers of the United States understood, States are supposed to serve the interests of the people; they are *not* the people themselves! States can be reborn but a race can *never* be reborn; once it is destroyed, it is gone for good.

Understanding all of this means a recognition that adulation of the United States, for example, while disregarding White people as a people, is a monstrosity. I have explained this in earlier pages but understanding what States really are heightens the realization. People who devote themselves to the United States are in essence devoting themselves to a *political* order and all too often fail to appreciate that raw devotion to a political order deflects their devotion away from where it most properly belongs: *their race*. No mere political order can possibly match our race in importance and indeed, the only real question worth asking in this regard is whether the current political order, whether that of the United States or that of other States, is conducive to the preservation of our White Race. If it is, wonderful. If it isn't, it behooves us to form a new one; it is as simple as that. Neither sentiment nor tradition can be allowed to deflect us from asking that basic question, for if the current States are *not* conducive to our continued existence as a race, what choice do we really have but to seek to form new ones, that is, if we wish to live? And nor are we merely concerned, of course, with the preservation of our lives as individuals but rather we are also concerned with *the life of our race*. We want our race to live on, *permanently*. We want the individual lives of White people to be preserved, certainly, but the life that we love goes far beyond that. What we love is our cultural, genetic, and biological *existence*, in sum, and so let us put the question in a slightly different way: are the present States of this world in which White people live conducive to the preservation of that cultural, genetic, and biological existence of White people, both as individuals and as a race? To break that question down, is the culture of White people preserved and secure in the present States of this world? Is our unique genetic existence preserved and secure in the present States of this world, that is, free from destruction through mongrelization with the other races? Lastly, are the very lives of our White people, their biological existence, preserved and secure in the present States of this world, that is, free from threat of death or injury at the hands of non-white attackers?

The answer to all of these questions is, quite plainly, no. We live in States that take no action whatever to preserve or secure

White culture or our genetic purity as a White Race and we furthermore live in States where literally millions of White people have been assaulted or murdered at the hands of non-white attackers. We live in States that practically *brag* about how little they care about the White Race as a race. We live in States that denounce, in fact, any and all attempts to preserve and secure White culture, White genes, and White lives. Some of the States that we live in around the world are, at best, raceless, while others are avowedly anti-White. Under neither scenario is our race preserved and secure. We live in States where White culture has practically been overwhelmed by that of the other races to the point where White people don't even know what their true culture is anymore. We live in States where "freedom" includes the "right" to mongrelize our race into oblivion. We live in States where non-white "immigrant" invaders are forced upon us no matter how destructive to our culture, our genes, and our lives. Not one government of any of these States is willing to pass *even one law* with the aim of preserving and securing the culture, genes, and lives of White people as a White people. An honest and rational man would have to admit all of this, friend and foe alike. There is no use debating these facts.

Is our White Race really being preserved and secured in its existence when, as a pitifully small percentage of the world's population, we don't even have a single State that we can call our own where our best interests are represented exclusively, where White people as White people are *cared* about? Is our White culture preserved through saturation with non-white culture, our White genes preserved when people are allowed to mongrelize them, and our White lives preserved when non-whites are free to kill them? I think not. Do you?

Whether the present States of the world are conducive to the preservation of our White Race may well be a question whose answer is so obviously no that it need not have been given such a detailed answer. And yet, we want the matter to be quite clear. Simply put, there exists *no* State today where the culture, genes, and lives of our White people are preserved and secure. Therefore, if we value that preservation and security, a new State must be formed, a Racial State. We who love White Life refuse to believe that the signers of the Declaration of Independence would not count that within the "life, liberty, and pursuit of happiness" that deserve securing by States. On the contrary, the eternal life, liberty, and pursuit of happiness of a race are necessarily far more important than that of the mere present *generations* of it. We in fact discern no State at all in this world that could have a higher purpose. Nation-states have existed in this world so as to preserve the nation in question and no one ever complained about that. Why then should it be different with our Racial State? This world is a vast place; are we really to believe that amidst the plethora of nation-states and multiracial States that presently abound, there is no room anywhere on the planet for a White Racial State? Is not the very notion yet again an illustration of hatred for White people, the type of hatred that makes the creation of a White Racial State all the more necessary, all the more valid? How long must we allow ourselves to be at the mercy of such hatred, hatred that would deny our White Race a State of its own so that it may live? If nations have a right to preserve themselves, as practically everyone would acknowledge, how can our White Race as a whole not have that same right? If something is granted to the nation, it cannot very well be denied to the race which is, after all, composed of many nations. We have the right to preserve and secure our White Race as much as there exists any right in this world. We have not called for the destruction of the multiracial States though we easily could and maybe should; instead, we merely call for the creation of a State where our race is *not* destroyed. Again, we either want the preservation of our race or we do not. If we do, we must necessarily oppose the current political order whereby our race is not preserved and secured and desire the creation of one where it is. We live or we die; there is no in between.

Today our White Race is in fact dying. If it were not, this book could never have been conceived, let alone written. The despoilment and humiliation of the White Race is everywhere. Our culture is being taken from us, our genes are being destroyed through rampant mongrelization, and we are being assaulted and killed by non-whites on an incessant basis. To create a Racial State that would end such a destruction of our racial life is thus justified by any decent moral standard and yet even if it weren't, we would *still* be entitled to work towards it simply because we find it far more desirable than the present situation. The "life, liberty, and pursuit of happiness" of our race is very much on our minds. Without the life of our race, there can ultimately be no liberty, and without the liberty of our race, there can ultimately be no pursuit of happiness, at least not in any form that we can deem worthwhile. We do not, for example, accept the idea that anyone has a right to a "liberty" that includes conduct that destroys our racial life. We do not, for example, accept the idea that anyone has a right to a "pursuit of happiness" that includes conduct that likewise destroys our racial life. Rather, within our Racial State, we want the fullest amount of liberty and pursuit of happiness *consistent* with that racial life, for it can never be just or proper to extol the liberty and pursuit of happiness of the individual at the *expense* of the race whose life of which the individual is merely a part. We lovers of White Life thus quite simply reject the idea that anyone, anywhere has a "right" to behave in a manner that harms that Life! And we further take notice that life is placed first *before* liberty and the pursuit of happiness in the Declaration of our forefathers. All of these forefathers were White men who observed racial distinctions. It is inconceivable that they would not want their White Race to survive or think that, if later generations of it came to the conclusion that the United States, or any other States for that matter, proved to be no longer conducive to that survival, that preservation, that *life*, we the White people of the world would not be free to work towards the formation of *new* States that are. "Life" must include the life of our race; "liberty" must include the freedom of our race to be itself, to live for itself, to advance itself, to protect itself, and preserve itself; and the "pursuit of happiness" must include what *we* find to be happy and, to be sure, we do not find the current anti-white order to be a happy one! We further know how much happier we will be and our descendants will be when we have a land of our own, *for* our own: our Racial State.

Let us state some additional, incontrovertible facts. In an exclusively White Racial State, White culture is necessarily preserved because that is the only culture present. In an exclusively White Racial State, White genes are preserved because those are the only genes present. In an exclusively White Racial State, White lives are preserved from being taken by non-whites. These facts are undeniable; we would challenge anyone to refute them. Instead, what we have today is the destruction of all. The choice between the destruction of all and the destruction of none is a stark one indeed that presents no doubt in our minds. In our White Racial State, our people will no longer be the slaves of non-white cultures, non-white mentalities because non-whites will simply not be part of the State. In our White Racial State, there will be no interbreeding of the races because there will be no other race present to interbreed with. In our White Racial State, thousands and millions of White lives will be spared from assault and murder because so many of the assaults and murders that currently occur are at the hands of non-whites. True, White people will still victimize *one another* but it is an inescapable fact that without non-whites present, there can be no non-white assault and murder upon *us*. What is amazing, on the other hand, is that anyone would really think that non-whites have a right to the opportunity to assault and murder us in the first place! Think about it, my Brothers and Sisters: if someone claims that non-whites have a "right" to be part of any State where White people live, he is, in effect, saying just that, for there can be no non-white opportunity to harm us unless they are in fact present amongst us. No presence means no harm; a right to presence means a right to the opportunity to do harm. We would rather deny them the "right" and the ensuing opportunity altogether. All one has to do is read the crime statistics of the past fifty years to know what rivers of our people's blood have been spilled at the hands of the non-whites. We want to stanch those rivers. If non-whites wish to kill each other, that is their business, but no one can deny us the option to seek a new state of affairs by which *we* are no longer killed by *them*: the Racial State. We owe it to our White people to provide them with this State.

It is noteworthy that were we instead to proclaim a desire to save the culture, genes, and lives of the non-existent "human" race that that would not be deemed controversial, and yet our desire to do so for the actually existing *White* Race is. The only explanation, as always, is that the minds of our White people have been in chains. We could yell "long live the human race!" all we want from the rooftop without receiving any criticism. Is that not so? We could win Nobel Peace Prizes for our commitment to the "human race." We could do any number of things for the so-called "human race" and expect ample praise from news media, governments, and others of the world and yet the minute we say "White" instead of human, a race that actually exists, everything previously lauded then becomes suspect, dreaded, and feared. Furthermore, blacks and browns can talk all they want about how much they wish to preserve and advocate for their respective races without any criticism forthcoming, as we know. The problem then, as always, is the self-hatred of our own White people; the very word and concept "White" is objected to! "Human" is fine but "White" is not. Why?

Let us turn the argument around then. If we were to grant that there really is a singular, monolithic "human race," isn't the White Race part of that human race so that if the preservation of the human race is a noble, just, and worthwhile endeavor, the preservation of the *White* Race must be one too? Thus, if men were to work towards the establishment of a State where the culture, genes, and lives of the "human" race were to be permanently preserved, why should *that* be viewed with favor but *our* working towards the establishment of a State where the culture, genes, and lives of our *White* Race are permanently preserved *not* be since we are a part of that very alleged "human race," are we not? Does not preserving the whole, in other words, justify preserving *part* of the whole as well? What inanity there is in denying us the option to preserve our White Race while affirming to us the option to preserve a (non-existent) monolithic human race! What inanity there is in deploring the one while lauding the other!

Perhaps I repeat myself but how could the righteousness of our cause be more clear? We wish to preserve the culture of our White Race as much as others wish to preserve the culture of the "human race." We wish to preserve the genes of our White Race as much as others wish to preserve the genes of the "human race." We wish to preserve the lives of our White Race as much as others wish to preserve human life. If a new State were to be necessary to preserve human culture, genes, and lives, its creation would be fought for without hesitation. Why then should there be any hesitation with us? If it is right to love humanity, it must be right to love a part of that humanity. If it is right to preserve humanity, it must be right to preserve a part, the White part, of that humanity. If it is right to have a political situation by which the culture, genes, and lives of humanity are preserved and secure, it must be right to have a political situation by which the culture, genes, and lives of the White part of that humanity are preserved and secure. If it is right to have a State for human beings, it must be right to have a State for White beings. The only way that this could be wrong is if White people were not to be deemed human beings. Surely though the degradation of our people has not yet reached *that* level? Surely we are not willing to scorn ourselves out of humanity altogether? If humanity is important, White humanity must be important too. Is that not so?

Think of all the effort that has been expended upon the human races throughout history. If only a tiny fraction of that had been spent upon the White Race *as a race* these years, we would not be in the predicament in which we now find ourselves. What an insane, horrible, and thus detrimental idea it has been that the (non-existent) "human race" is important, indeed of total importance, but that the White Race is somehow of *no* importance! Hence the United States are soon to become majority non-white; hence Europe is moving steadily in that direction; hence the minds of our people are polluted with alien, inferior non-white attitudes that degrade them as human beings; hence millions of our people have been assaulted and murdered; hence the blood of our kind has been mixed (and hence destroyed) with that of the other races. In sum, *our Life is destroyed when it is not recognized to have value.* The Racial State, on the other hand, affirms that it *does* have value. In fact, we lovers of White Life affirm that, of all of the forms of life that exist upon this earth, *our* Life is the most precious since it is, after all, *ours.* Why should we value other lives more than our own? Why should we plant trees for others while cutting down our own? Why should our hearts beat in other races' chests? We have a culture of our own. We Racial Loyalists may not praise all aspects of it but we love it because it is, indeed, ours! We have genes of our own. They are what makes us what we are as White people. We Racial Loyalists may not praise this particular gene or that but we love our genes, our racial genes, because they are, indeed, ours! Finally, we have the very lives of our own people. They may not be perfect but we Racial Loyalists love them because they are, indeed, ours! We do not want individuals of other races to take them at their whim and will! If there is any collective right at all in this world, it is surely the right to value the existence of one's own people and our culture, genes, and lives *are* that existence. And to value that existence means to value that which would preserve that existence: the Racial State. Since the other races are far more numerous than our own, let *them* worry about their own affairs while we instead work to create a political situation by which our *own* race is protected, preserved, and secured.

There is no moral or ethical argument then against the creation of our Racial State. There have been all kinds of States throughout history as we've seen. These States are a matter of choice for the people involved as we've also seen. Furthermore, no one can rationally argue that our White Race lacks the prerogative to preserve itself any more than the supposed "human race" lacks the prerogative to preserve *itself* since we are, after all, part of that supposed "human race"; in other words, since humanity has a right to preserve itself, the White Race has a right to preserve *itself*, simply. Hence whatever arguments there are to be made against the creation of our Racial State must have other sources. Let us then examine them—and refute them—in turn.

We have, as White people—Americans in particular—had our brains in a box for a long time and disdain of a Racial State will undoubtedly spring from that mentally claustrophobic condition as a result. There cannot, of course, even be any *consideration* by our people for the creation of a Racial State until the chains upon their minds have been broken, or at least loosened, but assuming that they are, what do we face as opposition to the idea? In sum, mere sentiment and a feeling that it would not be practical. In the end, however, the belief in its *necessity* must be made to trump both. Here, in the United States of America, there are now over 100 million non-whites amongst us. America is quite simply not what it was in the 1950s, unlike what the politicians insist on pretending. It has changed forever due to their treason in refusing to close the U.S.-Mexican border, their deliberate importation of millions of non-whites into the country in order to break the status of the White majority, and their desire to provide their financial backers with greater profits from the cheap labor. Soon their treason will have proved successful in that we will indeed no longer be a majority in these States. Things will only grow worse for us as that happens, for if things are bad for White people when they *still have relative power*, how can we expect anything else when that is no longer the case? The White middle class has already been in decline for a long time. Decent employment is in decline. Moral values are in decline. Education is in decline. The conservatives say that "our values" will trump the decline and that "America is the greatest country in history" no matter what the hell actually happens here. The liberals say, "who cares about values?" What neither seem to understand is that the America of their forefathers no longer exists. It has become so diluted as to defy all recognition as the place that it was. How can the Constitution possibly mean the same thing to blacks, who were enslaved under it, as to a White man? How can American traditions in general and "the good ole red, white, and blue" mean the same thing to blacks when for much, if not most, of their history as alleged objects of veneration, blacks considered themselves "oppressed" by them? How can the Declaration of Independence mean the same thing to an American Indian as to a White man when that document refers to Indians as "merciless savages" and when that document heralded the driving of the Indian off of the American continent? How can the English language possibly mean the same thing to a descendant of Japanese as to a descendant of Anglo-Saxons? How can the heroic stand at The Alamo possibly mean the same thing to a mestizo Mexican-American *whose ancestors were on the other side* as to a White Texan of many generations?

No matter how many parades are held for "Americans of all races," no matter how much talk there is of a supposed "shared history" by the politicians, no matter how much teachers try to convince a skeptical non-white student population that the "American dream was always for everybody," the simple fact of the matter is that our history is different, our experiences have been different, and our notions of what the future should be like are different too. The bottom line is that it was foolhardy to attempt to deracinate America in the first place, to make America raceless, because *the White Race is what created these United States of America in the first place and we did it in our image.* Now that our image is fading, the image of America that the politicians claim to love so much is fading too. As the non-whites become more and more numerous, they will become more and more assertive of their own will and best interests to such an extent that White people will finally have no choice but to do the same thing for themselves. Where then do our interests lie? In having a Racial State or States, States that are entirely White and devoted to that race. Those States need not have the same borders as those presently existing. Rather, the White people who still dominate in some swaths of the country can simply create new borders that coincide with those swaths. That touches upon the issue of practicality, to be sure, but history shows that when people really want something, almost nothing is beyond achieving. To be blunt, why should we give a fig whether the United

States of America continue to exist in their continued political form when the survival of our culture, our genes, and our very lives are at stake? So we no longer have fifty States. So what? For most of our history, we didn't have fifty States either. So what if the name of the union of States might end up being changed to something else? What's more important, our name or our existence as a race? Do the people exist for the States or do the States exist for the people? We lovers of White Life say the latter as people throughout history have done the same. No "values," as the conservatives would say, or "civil liberties" as the liberals would say, can possibly trump the *value* of our very *existence*.

As the United States become more and more non-white, they quite simply lose their value as political entities and lose whatever allegiance is owed to them. A black America is quite simply not what the Founding Fathers had in mind. An Oriental, Arab, Pakistani, Jewish America is quite simply not what the Founding Fathers had in mind. Divorcing the United States of America from the White Man, his culture, and his genes renders them, in effect, mere political abstractions. Yes, as Americans, we care about America but whether we should maintain the current political arrangement is, once again, an entirely different question. When the American Union becomes majority non-white as is certainly the forecast, how can White people look upon it the same way as we did when it was 85 to 90 percent White in 1950? When we drive through larger and larger stretches of the country where all of the business signs are in Mestizo Spanish, Chinese, Arab, and the like and where we will need an interpreter in order to function, how will we be able to feel that this is still the America of our forefathers? And if it *is* no longer the America of our forefathers, shouldn't we consider creating a new political order more desirable than what the present one has become? When we have to pack up and move over and over so as to continue living amongst our own kind, how can we not want a new political order that puts a stop to that situation? When more and more of us find ourselves working for businesses owned by Chinese, Korean, East Indian, and other non-white nationalities and foreigners at that, how can we feel that the country is what we want it to be? Do we not have a right to our *own* country?

Because America is so obviously being taken over, overrun, and dispossessed by other races including outright foreigners, the politicians and the media more and more sing the praises of "capitalism." No wonder, as our once great country has become a mere cash cow to milk dry! In other words, the more the American Union loses its White racial identity, the more that multiracial "diversity" is trumpeted and practiced upon the land, the more that it becomes all things to all people, the consequence is that the only thing left is that of *mere money-making*. Culture, genes, and lives give way to "markets." Primitive, personal self-interest for cash rules the day when there is no longer any other solidifying common denominator in the society; what is sad still is that our White American people have been falsely led into thinking that the United States were somehow founded on the principle of "capitalism" in the first place! The supposed common denominator of "loving freedom," for its part, is not enough to unify people because "freedom" entails different things to different people, as well as due to the fact that "freedom" simply means the absence of restraint which is hardly a recipe for the solidarity of a State! No, for we lovers of White Life, a union of States upon the basis of mere "freedom" is not good enough, especially since the present governments and courts of those States have declared by word and deed that that "freedom" includes the "right" to *destroy* our White culture, our genetic existence, and our very lives.

When our White Race was the overwhelming majority in these States and thus relatively protected in its continued existence, this problem did not seem so much a threat and we could pretend, perhaps, that no Racial State was necessary. The same goes for the States of Europe. Now though that both places are simply being overwhelmed with non-white invaders—or whatever else one may wish to call them—anyone who truly values the small minority of White people in this world must seriously think about the creation of a new political order that would safeguard their existence and on as permanent a basis as possible: the Racial

State. Our freedom to continue our racial existence upon this earth supersedes, as always, the existence of any governments, States, or unions of States that do not, as a matter of law, policy, or customs, value that racial existence. That said, that does not mean that we desire the break up of any governments, States, or unions of States if we can help it; rather, only that we must indeed break them up if we can't. In the United States for example, there are several States whose populations are nearly all White and thus, with a few changes of law and policies, they can with little difficulty indeed become Racial States with the same borders as exist today. The main prerequisite, as always, is that the thinking of our people change. If it does, and I predict that it in fact will, quite simply nothing is impossible for it. The key is having the will supported by the mind. That said though, that must include the will to defy edicts, from whatever source they may come, aimed at preventing the creation of our Racial States. In other words, we cannot allow ourselves to be bullied, coerced, or intimidated out of what must be done. The will of the people, our will, must prevail against all tyranny and tyrannies from whatever source.

As for the practicality of the migration of large numbers of non-whites away from our States, let us consider the fact that if it was practical for so many millions of non-whites to enter these places in the first place, there is no logical reason why the situation cannot be nearly as practically reversed. In other words, if the people could come, the people can go. All history is in fact the story of the migration of peoples. The Turks moved from what is now Turkmenistan to what is now Turkey. The Finns moved from the thereabouts of the Ural Mountains to what is today Finland. Manchuria used to be nearly uninhabited but now is densely populated by Han Chinese. *The entire Western Hemisphere* (the Americas) itself used to be uninhabited but is now inhabited by every race and people under the sun. Free White people, American Indians (from over the Bering Strait), and others went there willingly; black slaves of course did not. In any case, the very history of North and South America overwhelmingly demonstrates that the migration of many millions of people *is* possible and there is no reason why such migration cannot, in essence, *continue* to occur but simply in a different *direction*. In fact, one could argue that migration is the rule in history, not the exception. Jews migrated from Europe and elsewhere to form the State of Israel and many millions of Muslims and Hindus migrated so as to accommodate the then newly independent Pakistani and Indian States. Thus not only have there been migrations throughout history but there have also been migrations for the express *purpose* of forming new States. White people migrated to North America and formed colonies which later, of course, also became States. While the history of sub-Saharan Africa is obscure due to a lack of any written languages, undoubtedly there was much migration there as well. As for North Africa, there used to be no Arabs there at all while now, of course, Arab culture and language dominates and the people there are largely Arab themselves. White people, for their part, are often called "Caucasians" because we purportedly originated in the thereabouts of the Caucasus Mountains and then proceeded to spread over Europe and Western Asia and beyond. Thus obviously we ourselves have migrated greatly! American Indians, for their part, originated in Asia and crossed what was then a land bridge connecting Asia and what is today Alaska. (It is claimed that they did so in pursuit of wild game but regardless of the reason, they indeed migrated from someplace else and thus are no more "native" to America than any other race or people.) The bottom line then is that there is nothing novel, nothing unusual, and nor need there be anything sinister, about mass migration. Peoples have migrated for all sorts of reasons throughout history and there is no reason why we cannot, nor should not, facilitate migration, emigration to be exact, so as to create our Racial States. In fact, with modern means of transportation, it can certainly be done easier than by means of the mass caravans, sailboats, and horseback riding of the past!

This is one of the main reasons why knowing history is so important, for knowing history enables us to keep an open mind as to the vital possibilities of the *future*, our future; it is because people *don't* know history then that they would cavalierly dismiss the possibility that all-White States could be formed (or restored) from these United States and that Europe could become all-White once again. In essence, we have ruled out things due to a failure to realize and appreciate that they have happened before! The present has thus formed a misplaced limitation upon us. All it takes though is for us to have the mind and will and our Racial States shall come to fruition. Furthermore, we are talking about a state of affairs to work *towards*, not something that must happen overnight. Through law, policies, financial incentives, belief, instinct, and popular will, the day can and will come when there will be States that we can call our own exclusively and which will be devoted exclusively *to us*. And let us not overlook the fact that the non-whites may also want their *own* Racial States: States of, for, and by *them* the same way that ours will be for us and that this too will help facilitate the transfer of the non-whites in *our* States to *their* States. Indeed, with their ever growing numbers amongst us and throughout the rest of the world, that may be inevitable. The southwestern United States, for instance, are becoming so brown that some brown people have actually already called for them to be declared States for their brown "raza." If this indeed happens, brown people in other States may find that region to be a more desirable place to be than their present location. They may find that a magnet, in other words, and the same may happen with the other races where *they* predominate. Thus forming Racial States may end up being the desire of *all* races in America. With both push and pull, Racial States will form all the easier. Even with the minds of our White people in chains, *most White people would rather live around White people* and the other races would rather live among their own kind too for that matter. Thus the separation of the races into Racial States in America will be easier than perhaps thought at first glance. Cooperation with the other races to that end may in fact be possible and even likely. Once the artificially imposed "integration" of the races is done away with, nature will more readily take its course. As the old saying goes, birds of a feather (naturally) flock together. We simply have to realize that our Racial State is needed, and in fact possible, for us to work towards it and working towards it will, in turn, make it *likely*.

As for the world situation, China, for instance, is practically nearly already a Racial State since its population is more than 99 percent yellow and since it seems devoted, though not overtly, to that yellow race exclusively. It would thus be a very short step for it to become a Racial State under our definition. Japan and other Asian States are very nearly the same way. Indeed, the non-Whites are the overwhelming population in dozens of States throughout the world. Why then should our White people not be the overwhelming, indeed exclusive population, in some of our own? Especially since we are such a small population in the world? Indeed, quite plainly, it is because we are so few in numbers that the White Racial State is so necessary lest our culture, genes, and lives be submerged in the sea of color. Ask the Jews what it is like to be at the mercy of more numerous populations. It is because they (supposedly) wanted an end to such a situation that they formed their own version of the Racial State: the Jewish State. We can say then that if it is good for the Jews to have a Jewish State, it must surely be good for our White people to have a White Racial State likewise. And if a Jewish State could possibly be formed in a sea of Arab States and populations, the formation of our White Racial States will be all the easier in light of our much more favorable demographic situation. (There are far more White people in America and Europe than Jews in the Middle East). Thus yet another example in history points in our favor. The State of Israel has been called the homeland for the Jewish people. Whether it should have been formed where it is and under the circumstances it was are worthy points of strong debate but few people would challenge the idea that the Jews *should* have a homeland aimed at *preserving the Jews*. Likewise, we lovers of White culture, White genes, White lives—White Life—want a State to do the same thing *for us* and we should not logically find that proposition challenged either. To deny us a State though is, in effect, to challenge that proposition. Yes, unlike the State of Israel for the Jews, which has a mixed population racially, we who love White people want a State that is exclusively composed of our own race, and yet the point remains the same in both cases: the preservation of a particular group. We deem such racial exclusivity necessary for that preservation and so as to defeat, from the very outset, any claim that we are "oppressive" to anybody, a claim of course that has subverted us long enough already. In other words, it is not racial *separation* that causes oppression but rather it is racial *integration, for only when races are mixed together can one race oppress another*. This fact is undeniable.

It is not for any *other* race to decide what is necessary for *our* preservation any more than it is for *us* to decide what is necessary for *theirs*. The State of Israel, for its part, routinely follows that course of conduct: it refuses to obey the will of the so-called "international community" whenever it deems that will to be harmful to it and the Jewish people. It does so openly and forthrightly. While this exasperates the rest of the world, it is right for it to do so since the purpose of the State of Israel is the preservation of the *Jews*, not the rest of the world. It takes care of itself, letting the rest of the world take care of *itself*. It is right in that regard and so are we lovers of White Life for wanting our own State that does so for *us*. The fact that our White Race, though small, is far more numerous than the Jews (a people of several racial origins)—hundreds of millions more in fact—only justifies that we have our own State or States all the more. Unlike the Jews, after all, we are still, as an encyclopedia or dictionary would put it, "a major division of humanity," and yet amazingly, we currently have no State of our own! Instead, the States where we live are essentially being *colonized* by other races. By having a State composed exclusively of our race, we say, finally, that *here* no colony, a colony that would later burgeon into vines that would strangle us, will be allowed to take root in the first place. We do not wish to oppress but nor do we wish to be oppressed. We hence eliminate, under any viewpoint, the idea that we are either oppressive in our State or oppressed since there will be no other races in our State to either be oppressed or to do the oppressing. Thus those who hate "oppression" should obviously be in favor of the creation of our Racial State. Finally we can put an end to the oppression claims that go back and forth since an openly and obviously homogeneous State puts an end to such claims. The State of Israel, incidentally, will never be able to rid itself of such claims in light of its mixed population of Jews and Arabs and that mixed population will almost certainly, in due time, cause its downfall as a Jewish State. Quite simply, as the non-Jewish population grows there and the Jewish population decreases percentage-wise, the Jews will be required to become ever more oppressive in the eyes of its non-Jewish inhabitants while they struggle in vain to keep Israel a "Jewish State" altogether. We lovers of White Life must avoid such a mistake on *our* part. No, we will not use non-whites for cheap labor as the Israelis did and do with the Arabs. No, with us there will be no oppression even conceivable. We White people have learned the hard way what damage can be caused by cries of "oppression!" and thus avoid, with our Racial State, such damage from being repeated. We will neither oppress nor be oppressed. That must be our resolve.

We have called the State that we seek to create "the Racial State" mainly so as to be consistent and analogous in terminology with heretofore existing nation-states, city-states, and the "multiracial" States of today. It should be understood by now that there is nothing bizarre or outlandish about our desire for such a State and that any sentiment to the contrary is simply a reflection of the anti-White hostility that is so much a part of the political psyche of today. If there can be States devoted to a particular nation ("nation-states") without widespread controversy or criticism, as there have been throughout history and especially the 19th century, why should there not be States devoted to a particular race, Racial States? If there can be States today devoted to multiple races ("multiracial states") without widespread controversy or criticism, why should there not be States devoted to only one race, Racial States? There is no logical reason why a nation-state should be presumed valid but a Racial State should be presumed invalid. There is no logical reason likewise why a *multiracial* state should be presumed valid but a Racial State should be presumed invalid. Thus if you deem either the nation-state or the multiracial state valid, you must deem the Racial State likewise. It is no more reasonable to allow all races into a State, logically speaking, than to allow only one race into a State. It is no more reasonable to devote a State to the (professed) interests of all races, logically speaking, than to devote a State to the interests of only one race. Thoughts to the contrary are simply a prejudice. The prejudice has existed for awhile but it need not be permanent. Like all prejudices, it dissipates with education and reflection as well as due to circumstances that cannot be ignored.

What though is our vision for our Racial State? It is not enough, after all, to simply want one; for men to be moved to fight for its creation, they must have as complete as possible a vision of what it will be like. First though let it be clear that it is the task of White people everywhere, not just in America or Europe, to fight for its creation. Whether we are in America, Europe, Russia, Australia, or elsewhere, may we fight for its creation on as large a scale as feasible and desirable as the circumstances allow. The Whiter the current State, the easier it will be to become a Racial State. Thus current States like Iceland, Poland, Belarus, and the Baltic States whose populations are, unlike western, continental Europe, almost all White, have an excellent prospect of quickly transitioning into Racial States. As I have sought to make clear throughout this book, our struggle is not about geography, language, and nor about any particular ethnicity but rather is instead about our White people on this earth as a whole. Thus the message of Racial Loyalty and of the ensuing Racial States is for White people everywhere they may be found, whatever their ethnicity, and whatever their language. Whether we are in the Urals or in the Pyrenees, whether we are on the Great Plains of America or in the dry deserts of Australia or a hundred other places, may we White people fight for the creation of our Racial States. The bond that we have with one another is our *race* and so we Racial Loyalists wish for the successful creation of Racial

States amongst *all* of our White people no matter how much the particular ethnicity, language, and customs in question may happen to differ from our particular own.

We thus admit for the possibility that the character of each Racial State will differ in various respects from one another while retaining the two fundamental criteria that make a Racial State in fact a Racial State in the first place: 1) that the population of it be entirely White and 2) that the State be devoted exclusively to that race, specifically its continued cultural, genetic, and biological existence. All else can vary; there need be no more uniformity than that. It would be wrong in fact for us to insist that each Racial State mirror every other since that would be unnecessary for the preservation of our race and would intrude upon the unique customs, cultures, and traditions of the people who compose it. If one Racial State, for example, wishes to have a monarchical form of government, it is not for another Racial State to complain; if the people there determine that having a monarch would be most conducive to the preservation of White cultural, genetic, and biological existence, that is their choice. If another Racial State, for example, has laws that permit or forbid certain activities by the people that other Racial States do not permit or do not forbid, that too should not be a source of complaint by those other Racial States. What matters, simply, is that Racial States be Racial States. Some Racial States may choose to be republican or democratic; others may choose to be authoritarian. Some may adopt official religions; others may not. Some Racial States may, in the realm of economics, embrace a racially loyal free enterprise, others a racially loyal mixed economy, others something else still just as racially loyal. These are matters for each specific people to decide; *the only thing that must be true across the board is that the State, as a matter of open and avowed policy, be entirely White and devoted to the White Race.* When you think about it, that is actually very little to ask. Gone must be the idea that one State of White people should impose its will upon another State of White people. Rather, we are all Brothers and Sisters with our own desires within the context of our racial preservation. That context itself though can and must never change. Much is possible within that context; little is required. If we must be ruthless in any respect, it must be for the maintaining of the context itself as the survival of our cultures, genes, and lives absolutely depend on that. Such a context can never be negotiable, naturally enough, under any circumstances. We will neither barter nor beg for the life of our race; we will assert it absolutely. The governments of our Racial States will reflect that reality in whatever particulars they are composed.

That said, there is no doubt that our Racial States will be *inclined* to have certain characteristics simply as part of the resolve to preserve our White Life. For example, I envision each State developing a constitution that proclaims itself a Racial State with that being unalterable by any lawful political process in the future. In other words, I foresee each Racial State being codified as a Racial State by law, law that at least *legally* can never be changed. While not foolproof, this will provide some protection for our States as Racial States against momentary—but dangerous nonetheless—whims to make them otherwise which likewise would endanger our racial life. I further foresee there eventually being only one political party in each Racial State; since our White Race is our *unity* and we are in fact all White, it seems superfluous for our White people to continue to be *divided* into different political parties. Rather, I foresee there being only one Racial Loyalist party in each State, whatever its exact name, within which our White people will work for their political benefit. Contrary to what may be popularly believed, it is actually better to have a one party political system than a two party political system because a two party system results in a divided, schismed people at odds with itself. Americans, especially today, know that as much as anyone. Emphasis is unfortunately taken away from the needs of the people to the needs of the *party;* politics in its noble sense is replaced with *partisanship.* People go to voting booths and essentially *cancel each other out* with their votes. The pendulum swings back and forth every so many years with no real benefit either way. Since the guiding principle of the White Racial State is White Racial Loyalty, a single party can fulfill that principle standing alone and it is difficult to understand why a two party or even a multiple party system would be desirable or deemed necessary. How would the unity of White people be helped or furthered by having more than one political party always at odds with one another? That is a fair question. It seems instead preferable to have one Racial Loyalist party so that every political viewpoint, whatever it may be, may be propounded within that basic context which is, after all, the context of the Racial State itself. That way, candidates for various political offices or positions will not be chosen on the basis of *party* but rather on the basis of the man himself. In other words, take away any difference of political party and the focus instead reverts to *the man*, his character, his qualifications, and his aims for the office or position. This is actually what George Washington and other Founding Fathers of the United States had intended for those States in the first place.

It is not too much to ask that each office or position seeker in the White Racial State be loyal to his White Race with every other matter of viewpoint being within that context. Thus, since all will necessarily be loyal to that race, one Racial Loyalist party will encompass all political activity, that party having room for all of the varying viewpoints within that context. In other words, we as individuals may disagree on various points but since we are all Racial Loyalists in Racial States, we need have no more than a single Racial Loyalist Party. Thus I foresee that each Racial State will eventually contain only one political party, a Racial Loyalist Party whose guiding principle is simply the same as that of the Racial State itself. The question may be asked though, why should there be any political party at all if the idea is to end the practice of voting for a party over the man? In other words, if one political party is preferable to two or more, why should no parties at all not be preferable to one? The answer is that there must be an active, organized, permanent body dedicated to the maintaining of the State as a Racial State.

The quality of life in our Racial State will be greatly improved, in every respect, over that which we are forced to endure today.

Education will be improved, for example, because it will no longer be dumbed down in the schools in order to accommodate the lower intellectual ability of the non-whites. (There can be no doubt that this has actually happened wherever and whenever White students are educated alongside black and brown students.) Thus with all-White classes in all-White schools, our White youth will be finally able to reach their true potential, challenged at a level not so easily met. They will be challenged at the *highest* level of those White students in the class rather than at the lowest (black and brown) level in the class which is what we have today. Our educational performance will thus reach the unparalleled level that it used to have, unmatched in the world. No longer will the first half of each year be spent relearning what was learnt the year before. It is not a coincidence that the educational performance of our White youth has plunged in comparison with the Asian countries in exactly those areas where the black and brown races have the most trouble—science, math, and reading—since the lessons have to be made easier in order to pass black and brown students. Without their presence therefore, our performance will rebound. No longer, furthermore, will our students' energy be squandered on the anti-White propaganda, nor in obeisance to "equality." Rather, the commitment will simply be to *Racial Loyalist excellence*. Excellence and "equality" in education are, and always have been, a contradiction in terms. Our students will know, yes, that they are all equally part of our White Racial Family but they will also be taught that the quest for *merit* is a sign of personal value that is worth attaining for its own sake and not just for the sake of a particular grade or a particular job prospect. All students should compete with one another and there should be no booby prize for those who fail. Instead of giving all of the students A's and B's practically by virtue of simply showing up, grades should be distributed over the entire spectrum with the average grade being a "C" since C is, after all, indicative of an average performance. It makes little sense to give an average student above average grades. Nor does it make sense for teachers to feel compelled to pass students who are simply unable "to make the grade." Due in part to the adulation of "equality," we live today in a "feel good" society in which failure is basically coddled and excused. I envision that such a thing will come to an end with our Racial State.

In the realm of employment, I envision that the wages of all employees will rise. This is because the previous, heretofore presence of the non-whites amongst us depressed our wages as is commonly known. Simply put, when employers can hire non-whites at lower wages than White people, they will either do so or force the White people themselves to accept lower wages if they are to be employed at all. As with educational performance, we have seen this negative impact of the presence of non-whites borne out by statistics: the more non-whites there are in any community, the lower are the wages in comparison with all-White or nearly all-White communities. Throughout history, non-whites have been willing to work for a lower wage thus undercutting the employment of our people. This is because, for whatever reason, non-whites are satisfied with a lower standard of living than White people. Thus when employers have the choice of hiring non-whites at a lower wage or Whites at a higher wage, they naturally tend to hire the non-whites so as to increase their profits. This in turn forces White people to accept a wage lower than they would otherwise lest they be unemployed. (If it were not for the minimum wage laws, the disparity would be even more striking and obvious.) Hence in our Racial State, without the presence of any non-whites, our wages will go up since our employers will have no choice but to hire *White* people, and at good wages at that, which will accommodate our higher standard of living. Yes, the profits of some employers will, in all likelihood, not be as high as they are today but that is too bad. Who ever said or came up with the idea that any White man has a right to employ cheap, non-white labor in the first place? White employers should employ White people, period, and it is not too much to ask that they do so at a decent wage that accommodates a decent standard of living. When all of the potential employees are White, an employer will either offer a decent wage or nobody will be willing to work for him. Thus the wage will be commensurate with the type of *labor* rather than with the type of *laborer* which is the case today. Incidentally, we deny that any White employer has the "right" to remove his business from the State so as to avoid paying his fellow White people a decent wage and the day will come when schoolchildren will be amazed to learn from their teachers that such a thing indeed once happened in the past. Every man deserves the fruit of his labor but we cannot see how any White man has the right to deny his fellow White men their labor altogether. Let there be profits and let there be work but let both be within our own racial household. The opportunity of one White man to add millions or even billions of dollars to the millions or billions he already has cannot outweigh the opportunity of many White men to have decent employment at decent wages.

In a State where the focus is on the culture, genes, and lives of our White *people* as a *people*, it is to be expected, quite naturally, that there will be less emphasis on materialism in general. When *race* is the Sun of our universe, the "star" of *cash* will not shine so brightly. Rather than every single activity being expected and devoted to the making of money, as is largely the case today around the world in the States where our race currently lives, other values will be asserted. I envision that those values which are a credit to our race, rather than merely for the personal benefit of the individual, will have prevalence. In a State where culture has such a profound importance, it is doubtful, for instance, whether the degradation of it will be tolerated no matter how much cash is part of the picture. Perversion sells in a society that has no enforced values except the making of money but in a society where the health of the *race* is paramount, the making of money will likely no longer be at the expense of the race's health, both mental, physical, ethical, and moral. Furthermore, the very fact that our State will be entirely composed of White people will mean a much more ethical and moral culture itself, for it is no coincidence that in America, for example, the increase of the non-white population has been matched by its ethical and moral decline. When a State is populated by different races, there can be no common ethical and moral values because each race inherently has a different idea as to what they should be. Hence when America, for instance, became "multiracial," ethical and moral values went into decline and they will continue to do so the more multiracial it becomes.

Values of honor, integrity, and self-sacrifice will return due to the creation of our Racial State. Each man and woman will have a keen sense that he or she is a representative of the Race to which ultimate allegiance is owed and thus will tend to comport himself or herself in such a way as to bring credit to that race. This stands in stark contrast to the current society in which the word "allegiance" has practically lost all meaning altogether, except perhaps in regard to the maniacal pursuit of personal wealth without regard to the damage inflicted upon society as well as upon the individual himself. When money is the dominant force in a society, it is to be expected, after all, that values such as honor, integrity, and self-sacrifice will erode since money can be made, and often can *only* be made, without any regard for such values at all. To put it simply, trash *sells* but with "selling" no longer being the focal point in the Racial State that we mean to create, there will be less *trash*, too. One simply cannot expect to have a moral and ethical society where society is viewed as a "market" where everything, including honor, is up for sale. It is little wonder that perversions have proliferated in the current society when the only yardstick is whether something will, or will not, "sell"! This is because perversions *always* sell and so if the only issue is whether there is money to be made, there will always be perversions ready to be fulfilled and coddled for financial gain. Thus, to want an ethical and moral society, while at the same time wanting the "market" to decide everything, is a hopeless contradiction. It is only a matter of time before religious so-called "capitalists" come to terms with this fact. Religion, for its part, is well aware that when man is left to his own individual devices, it is inevitable that he will be more savage than human; thus religion has always tried to give man a higher purpose, a purpose other than his own gratification which is all too often fulfilled through the debasement of self and others. The Founding Fathers of the United States had dim regard for human nature too and sought, at least at the federal government level, to keep man in "check." One simply cannot have any kind of meaningful community when the only consideration is individual self-interest, individual gratification, and individual greed. We see that everywhere in the current society, a society where people can see others hit by cars and feel no impulse to help, a society where people will do practically anything, no matter how idiotic, if the price is right, and a society where even the rape of *children* is tolerated so as to prevent possible damage to the lucrative *football* program at a well-known university, for example. I envision that the Racial State will sweep such things aside. The health of the Race comes before all individual desires in disregard of that health. Let the greatest of individual desires be fulfilled consonant *with* that health. When we lovers of White life say that we wish to preserve our people's cultural, genetic, and biological existence, we are not talking about a culturally, genetically, and biologically *inferior* existence! We are not talking about an existence where everything goes! Rather, we are talking about an existence that is not only intact but also *great*. To love our Race is to abhor the *defilement* of our Race: culturally, genetically, and biologically. Just as a son does not wish to see his mother prostitute herself, we, the sons and daughters of a great people, do not wish to see the defilement of that people. Rather, we want a superior culture, superior genes, and superior lives and we naturally mean to have them.

When the day comes when our White people no longer view themselves as detached "individuals" but rather as Brothers and Sisters of a racial family, can there really be any doubt but that they will be less inclined to rape, rob, and murder one another? Can there really be any doubt that they will, in general, treat one another better? When our individual selves are no longer the be all and end all of our existence, can there really be any doubt but that preoccupation with individual joys and pains will give way to a higher purpose in life? Can there be any doubt but that when hearts beat with that same purpose that the brotherhood of man, so desired in vain throughout the ages, may finally be attained? And not a brotherhood of mere *ideas* that is in fact unattainable because of conflicting views of those ideas but rather a brotherhood of blood which brooks no argument! And man not as a mere dollar sign in the eyes of others but of worth precisely because the beholder too is of worth for the same reason: as mutual members of the same racial family! Thus I envision our Racial State as being one of far less violence, strife, abuse, fraud, pornography, and dishonesty than is the case with the States of today due to the simple fact that these things are harder to inflict upon those whom you consider your family. How many brothers and sisters kill one another, for instance? How many brothers and sisters have strife with one another, abuse one another, defraud one another, display one another in sexually perverse photos, and lie to one another in comparison with that of "strangers," in the heart and mind, doing these things to one another? We can make no claim that the Racial State will be perfect but we *can* make the claim that it will be much better than what we have today. We can make no claim that there will not be pain and suffering in our Racial State but we *can* make the claim that there will be much less of it. When every White man, woman, and child is viewed as *kin*, as belonging to the same *kind*, they will treat one another with more *kind*ness. When we have a State in which our people are no longer viewed as mere accidents, nuisances, or dollar signs but rather as members of the same racial *family*, with care and consideration given to them accordingly, so much of the destruction of today will wither away. The "brotherhood" of all races, for its part, never worked because those of different race are so obviously *not* brothers; since they are obviously not of the same kind, their supposed "brotherhood" was patently false and the idea was a total failure. With our Racial State, on the other hand, such will not be the case since all White people do have kinship. There is much to clean up in our race to be sure but it will be done with a pleasant attitude, the attitude of racial love rather than the attitude of personal caprice.

Viewing society as a "market" can never match that of viewing society as a racial, organic community and let there be no mistake as to our preference for the latter over the former. Placing supreme value in cash conflicts, and always will conflict, with the placing of supreme value in race. Money is at best a *tool* but like all tools is subordinate to he who *wields* that tool. And how could we wish any differently? We lovers of White Life know that great damage has been done to our race due to the overemphasis placed on the pursuit of money. How many non-whites have been allowed into our lands because of the pursuit of larger profits by those who dangle politicians from the ends of their strings? How many of our people's minds have been corrupted by the sexual perversion in society because that perversion "sells"? How much of our racial bloodstream has been polluted because we have interbred with non-whites who enticed us with their wealth? How many of our young people feel a sense of hopelessness because they have been deceived into thinking that vast personal wealth is the primary goal in life since they know that goal will, in fact, elude them? If great personal wealth is the primary goal of each individual, it is all too easy to sacrifice that which is in the best interests of our race as a whole and this has been done repeatedly to this day. There is no escaping that reality. Our workers have been thrown out of work. When they do work, they are forced to "compete" with non-whites here and everywhere else in the world. Drugs are peddled to our people likewise for profit and the so-called "criminal justice system" profits by them too. Politicians do the bidding of the wealthy no matter how badly their White Race is hurt in the process because that obtains for them that primary goal of personal wealth as well as power. We have rated the quality of a man by how much money he has in his pockets rather than by his character, his honor, his ethics, and his morals. How then can we be surprised by the degradation of the present society? Parents sell their children. Lawyers seek "justice" for their clients but only if they are paid a large fee of several hundred dollars an hour. Doctors will leave operating materials in a man's chest if they cannot charge for removing them. People are paid to lie in commercials as a matter of course. Students incur massive debt so as to attend colleges that purport to guarantee high future income rather than actually bestow an exceptional education, while education itself is considered only an economic enterprise. No matter how extravagant the income, we have the temerity to say that the individual "earned" it. Why? Because he *made* it? Such is the misplaced value of today. We have the quantity of *cash* rather than the quality of *man*.

The bottom line is that the seeking of personal profit is rarely itself conducive to the health of White culture, genes, and lives and since *these* are the priority of the Racial State, I foresee the diminishing of the drive for personal profit in our Racial State accordingly. It will still exist, of course, as it is natural and right for a man to seek his own benefit. However, that drive for personal benefit will be kept within healthy bounds by the duty we all owe to our White Race itself. It is a duty owed by virtue of our membership in that race and it is a duty that can never be canceled.

Can there be any surprise then that we who long for the Racial State, for the State where supreme value rests with the health, weal, and yes, profit, *of our race as a whole,* envision that the degradation of today's society described earlier will not be present in the State that we mean to create? That the days of treason, embarrassment, perversion, and idiocy will be over? Where men and women will stand on their *quality* rather than their quantity? Where we shall receive the fruits of our labor but will never degrade *ourselves* with our labors? Where a man's word will be his bond no matter how unprofitable to his person the keeping of it might be? Where there is more appreciation for the honest auto mechanic than for the dishonest multi-millionaire? Where our people will be unwilling to make imbeciles out of themselves no matter how much it could pay? Where a man's "worth" will not be determined by his finances but rather by a look at the man himself and his loyalty to his White people? Where the honorable life will take precedence over the materialist life? Where a man will look into a mirror and say to himself, "I do not only exist for myself but rather do I exist also for my family and my racial family, wherever it may be! No trinkets divert me from that love, nor shall they!"? This I envision in the Racial State that we work towards, the Racial State of tomorrow.

I envision a more social society, a more personal and loyal society, with less emphasis on technology in favor of personal bonds, where a look into the eyes and the hearing of another's voice will mean more than it does today, a society where these bonds will be cultivated with considerable attention and seriousness. I envision a society where our people will seek to plant deeper roots in their communities and disdain moving about accordingly; a less mobile society and happily so, where their neighbors will not be strangers and where their neighborhoods will be well known to them. In these respects, our Racial State will thus look more the way States *used* to look. In a State where race is the fundamental criterion of identity, of unity, of brotherhood, where roots are much valued and economic activity is not guided solely by individual financial gain, there will be less impetus for our people to move about than there is today. With the victory of that which we have in common, our race, we will have a greater sense of *community*. Instead of feeling like "atoms" as we do in the present polyglot, purposeless multiracial States, we will each have a sense that we have personal value and that we have a role to play in our race's present and future. More children will go to the same schools that their parents went to, their grandparents went to, and beyond. Our people will have more of an awareness of whom their ancestors were and more of a consideration of who will be their descendants. There will be a greater understanding that the present generation is the link between past and future and that we need that link to be as strong as possible to ensure that that future will be a great one. Rather than chaos there will be order. Rather than randomness there will be purpose.

Why should there be shame in living in the same neighborhood, going to the same schools, and even living in the same homes as our forefathers? There is something to be said for such roots as much as they are presently denigrated. Many of us in the present have lost such roots because our neighborhoods have been overrun by those not of our race and because the present economic system (that we have basically allowed to dominate our lives) has moved us around to "wherever the work is" as if we were nomads. Obviously with the Racial State the first mentioned problem will be a thing of the past. As for the second, I believe it too will be passed because I envision that in a State guided by race, economics will be subordinate. Rather than a master of what we can do and cannot do, it will be a tool to help ourselves. Rather than a straitjacket, it will be our plow. Thus, for example, if the government of our State wishes to invest in the creation of a factory in an isolated community so as to provide work for the populace, there is no reason why it shouldn't. Under the present way of thinking, such an idea might be considered well-nigh blasphemy to a supposed "free market" but in a State devoted to the welfare of our race, what can be wrong with making sure that our brethren have work, that they *don't* abandon their communities, their roots, in all too often fruitless searches for work in the big cities? If the present United States can squander literally trillions of dollars on useless wars overseas and "foreign aid," surely our Racial State can help its own people where it is needed, on occasion? Again, should we serve the economics or should the economics serve *us*? Should we be the slave or should we be the master? Where is the sense in taking the money of our people and squandering it on other peoples, whether directly or indirectly, but crying foul at the idea of using the money of our people to help *ourselves*? Where is the sense in avowing the power of the State to do the former (helping the people of other States) but denying the power of the State to do the latter (helping the people of our own State)? In our Racial State I envision rather that matters will be the other way around and, in particular, foresee the end to wasteful wars that come about generally because of the bizarre idea that the way other races live their lives is somehow our business.

That of course brings up yet another benefit of the Racial State over the mess with which we are currently afflicted: the end of wars which occur out of the misplaced idea that the welfare and doings of the other races are things that we should be concerned with. They aren't. Rather, they are the concern of the races involved. Thus a Racial State would never have gone to war in Korea, in Vietnam, in Panama, in Iraq, and other places less publicized. Thus with the advent of our Racial States, we put an end to wars that only bankrupt our own people and kill us and the other races to no benefit at all for our own White Race. With the advent of the Racial State, we put an end to policing and guarding the world, instead preferring to police and guard *ourselves*. If a State of Arabs is under a "ruthless dictator," that is none of our business. If a State of Orientals is communist, that is none of our business. If a tribe of African blacks is killing another tribe of African blacks, that is none of our business. It is not our task to impose our will or desires on races not of our own but rather to take care of ourselves; thus instead of the current attitude of supremacy over others there will be the attitude of self-maintenance. Do not bother us and we will not bother you. You are on your own and we are on our own too. Neither the master nor the slave of other races; neither the oppressor nor the oppressed. Let our destiny not be tied to any other race, nor their destiny tied to ours. That is true freedom for which we fight, a freedom that respects our difference as different races rather than demands our mingling, merger, and consequent destruction. Thus rather than the situation we have today with the United States, for example, which have over 800 military bases in 130 foreign States around the world so as to interfere in other people's business and defend them or attack them at a moment's notice, our Racial States will take care of *themselves* which is the best course of action for those who desire true peace.

It perhaps goes without saying too that the best hope of peace between *White* people is the Racial State as well. In a State where the focus is placed upon the cultural, genetic, and *biological* life of our White people, can anyone really believe that our Racial States will have any inclination to war with one another, thus destroying that life? Had the States of Europe and America been Racial States in the 20th century, there could not have been the horror of the First and Second World Wars. Indeed, had the

States of Europe and America been Racial States throughout history, untold hundreds of millions of our White people would not have lost their lives and we would accordingly not be the small and crowded population (compared with the other races) that we are today. Think of the suffering that could have been avoided! Think of how much more territory our White people would inhabit on this earth had we not slaughtered each other over the scraps of Europe instead! In a State where the focus is on race instead of nationality, the best interests of that race obviously take priority over that of any nationality. Thus wars between nations of the same race become a thing of the past since such wars are so obviously harmful to the *race*. An attack of one White nation upon another would be viewed instead as an attack upon one's own *race*, something anathema to the entire purpose of the Racial State. Indeed, such an attack would be perceived as an attack upon *one's own people* since race, not nationality, would be the defining character of the State. Why do wars between the different nationalities of a race occur? Because the particular nations in question think that such wars will benefit their *nations*. If such a benefit is no longer the issue though, replaced instead by a desire for *racial* benefit, such wars can no longer occur because all wars of White people against White people obviously and automatically *hurt* White people. White people as *White* people do not benefit by their killing one another, quite simply, whereas a *nationality* might benefit by doing this to another *nationality*. Nor would there be such a thing as "victory" in such wars because there is only one victory for the Racial State: *racial* victory. When one examines the Second World War, for example, one can discern that various *nationalities* obtained victory, true, but nobody can declare that the conflict was a victory for *White* people. The death of tens of millions of White people is no victory for White people. The conquest of one White State by another White State is, in fact, a loss. When bombs fell on Warsaw during the Second World War, we lost. When bombs fell on Berlin, we lost. When bombs fell on London, we lost. When bombs fell on Moscow, we lost. That is because our "we" is our *race*, not our respective nationalities. Nationalities might have won this or that (and even that is doubtful) but the *race* lost because the race was at war with *itself*. I thus envision that a Racial State, a State devoted to our race in all respects, will quite simply be unwilling to war with that race. Since our race transcends all borders, there will be little incentive to expand the borders of this or that nationality. Since all wars between White people are hostile to White Life—and since the purpose of the Racial State will *be* White Life—there can be no more wars between White people in the Racial State.

Our outstretched hands joined in brotherhood transcend the lines on maps; our love of race avoids the destruction of race through war. A State that is determined to preserve White culture, White genes, and White lives cannot countenance warfare's destruction of same. Thus the Racial State will put an end, finally, to the age-old intraracial warfare perhaps like no other fact or force has ever been able to in the history of the world. When Helen of Sparta decided that she wanted to become Helen of Troy, in Homer's *Iliad*, no Racial State would have deemed the matter as even remotely justifying a war between those two great White States. A thousand other examples could likewise be cited if the matter were not already so obvious: when White people view themselves and identify themselves by that genetic reality and see the very purpose of the State as the preservation of it regardless of any political borders, all wars between White people come to an end since war itself between White people violates the very purpose of the Racial State.

Likewise, with a State that is devoted to White Life, we can expect less of a willingness to destroy that Life *within* the State. Just as our people will be less inclined to kill one another through crime or war, they will be less inclined to kill their unborn children through (misnamed) "abortion." Abortion ends both a genetic line as well as ends life and thus I envision that in a State that is devoted to both genes and lives that such destruction of genetic lines and lives will, if not end entirely, be much lessened. It is little wonder that abortion makes sense in a society that is entirely focused on the *individual* but *doesn't* make sense in a society focused on the *race*! And nor is this merely a matter of governmental power either but rather it is one of *attitudes*. If a woman looks upon her unborn child as entirely hers without any significance outside of the impact upon her own individual life, it is little wonder that she may deem it desirable to end her pregnancy should she think that impact to be a negative one. On the other hand, should she look upon her unborn child as a future son or daughter of her *race* too, that her child belongs not just to her but also to her *race*, she will be less inclined to kill it or even imagine the thought of doing so. Thus yet again, the racial view of life, as represented by the Racial State, saves lives. I further envision that in our Racial State the act which causes pregnancy in the first place will be looked upon with far less flippancy and carelessness than it is today and so this too will reduce the amount of "abortions" with which we are presently confronted. In a State avowedly devoted to the culture, genes, and lives of its White people, there will be more regard for and attention paid to actions in general. With sexual relations in particular, there will be a greater tendency to think about the possible consequences beyond the act itself, consequences that not only accrue to the individual but also to her race.

In a State where culture is no longer seen as a mere accident but rather as something to consciously *cultivate*, I envision a renaissance ("rebirth") of high culture in that State. I envision that fine art, music, and architecture will return and will consciously and deliberately, with the support of the State itself, crowd out the decadent "culture" with which we are confronted today. That which is alien to our people will be recognized for what it is and will wither, accordingly, in a State that is devoted to the culture of its own people. For example, I can foresee the return of classical music and art education to the public schools as well as State support of high culture in general. We must reject the notion that the State should be neutral in matters of culture; rather, the State should be the rigorous champion of all that which is great. Uncultivated culture is like a garden that is being strangled by weeds. Cultivated culture, on the other hand, is like a garden where all that is worthwhile blossoms. The Racial State, devoted to White culture as it is, will inevitably have a higher regard for culture than do the current States by virtue of that very fact. And it *is* possible to say that some cultural achievements are superior to that of others. High culture is today smothered in the present States because that which is inferior *always* vastly outnumbers that which is superior. Thus the superior, the actual fruits and vegetables of the garden, must have special support lest they be submerged by the weeds. As any gardener knows, an uncultivated garden means a "garden" that is overcome by weeds! And the prevention of this, I believe, will be the outlook of the Racial States of the future. Today most of our White people have little exposure to high culture at all simply because they are swamped by inferior culture. It is little wonder then that they embrace the inferior culture for that is all they see around them. I envision that matters will be altogether different in the Racial State. Education will not be geared to make our children good future "consumers"—a degrading term at best—but rather will be geared to build their minds, their bodies, their skills, their ethics, and their character. High culture, the culture that most truly is a credit to our race, will play a significant part in that effort.

Consider the situation today where the federal government of the United States always has plenty of money to spend on million dollar bombs and billion dollar airplanes but the schools within those States don't even have the modest resources to pay for any school music or art programs. Consider the situation today where culture is guided exclusively by personal financial considerations and nothing else! I envision that priorities will be very different in the Racial State. To have the means to defend one's State is one thing, but to forsake the betterment of *one's own people* in the process is quite another. The Racial State will be more concerned with *bettering* the lives of its citizenry than with *ending* the lives of those in other States, it is fair to say. It is also fair to say that, in a State where culture is considered so important, whether someone will personally profit financially by this or that cultural achievement will largely be beside the point. Rather culture will be cultivated and supported for its own sake, with its best creators and purveyors receiving whatever assistance from the State they need so that they may be able to focus exclusively on their noble pursuits. May the next Mozart, Michelangelo, and Rembrandt be found! May we have a State that has the means to discover, encourage, and sustain them in their labors so as to make the world a more beautiful place! Greatness is not induced by a "market' any more than nobility is induced by a mob. Rather, it is the duty of the Racial State to use its power to foster such greatness. This is really nothing new for historically, States did just that; States subsidized the great composers, architects, artists, and writers and let it be that way again. The Racial State will reserve the right to distinguish between sumptuous fruit, the genius of our kind, and the willy-nilly, worthless weeds that have always been the rule rather than the exception. It is the *fruit* that has always needed the help while the weeds have always done just fine when left to their own devices. Who indeed ever heard of the growth of fruit endangering the weeds in a garden? Rather, it is, of course, the other way around. May our Racial States of the future cease being neutral bystanders and readopt the traditional role of States as protectors of cultural genius, for cultural genius is the greatest treasure of every people aside from the genes and lives of the people themselves.

I envision there being far fewer laws on the books in our Racial States because the multiplicity of laws that we are currently burdened with is largely a result of an attempt to bind multiple races and cultures together within the same State. Since the multiracial State is totally diverse, in other words, law is used as a proxy for the absence of a common race, culture, and values; since the society is not held together by any common background of its citizens, nor of their viewpoints, governments feel compelled to pass in that absence ever more laws instead in order to hold the society together. In homogeneous societies, on the other hand, the people feel a bond with one another that discourages the type of societal mayhem that we witness in multiracial societies and thus less laws are necessary as a means of preventing such mayhem. Thus our Racial State will not need a dozen different laws against killing someone, or defrauding someone, or stealing from someone because people consciously bonded by blood quite simply have less of a motivation to do these things. There are few laws on the books in Japan, likewise, because nearly everyone is Japanese and is of the same race and culture. Here in America, on the other hand, laws abound regulating, criminalizing, and codifying practically everything and the laws that are already on the books never seem to be enough as far as the politicians are concerned. Instead, the statute books grow thicker every year. There are more and more courts, more and more judges, and more and more lawyers. Aristotle said more than 2,300 years ago that when there are many doctors and lawyers in a society, it is a sign that the society is sick and criminal. He was right. We Racial Loyalists would rather be bound by our blood and our White culture than by a proliferation of laws which would merely restrain ourselves outwardly but without affecting our basic attitudes. With one, racial code of ethics in our Racial State, there will accordingly be less of a need for laws as a means of forcing us to behave in an ethical manner. Thus many of the laws that exist in America today, for instance, would end, their being superfluous in our Racial State. There will be less of a bureaucracy to enforce and promulgate laws as well.

Yes, there will always be a need for law. However, more laws is not necessarily better and as stated, the multiracial State by its very nature requires a proliferation of laws and with less and less freedom, accordingly, the more multiracial it becomes. I envision that our Racial State would rather say, "I treat you well because you are a fellow White man" than "I treat you well because there is a law that would punish me if I did not." The first is a stronger sentiment; the second is a matter of mere selfish expediency that is easily thrown aside if "the law" is looking the other way. Of course things would not be perfect in our State but then again, they never are, but to have a State where people feel bound by racial brotherhood is always preferable to having a State where the main motivator for conduct is simply the avoidance of criminal or civil penalty.

In every respect, the Racial State that we envision will be better than the States that exist now. Without the presence of the other races, there will be far less crime, overwhelmingly so, since so much crime is at their hands. Our people will be able to walk the streets anywhere and everywhere in our State and without fear. Without the presence of the other races, we will have a better educational system and one that ends the false guilt complex with which we are currently afflicted. Without the presence of the other races, we will have a higher culture once again. Without the presence of the other races, we will have full employment and at good wages. Without the presence of the other races, there will be less of a need for laws—hence restricting our freedoms—since our race will be a form of law unto itself. Without the presence of the other races, we will have a more moral and ethical society. With the Racial State, there will be less war and less social strife. With the Racial State, there will be no more political partisanship and there will be less political corruption. With the Racial State—where economics has been put in its place as our *servant* rather than as our master—we will have cleaner air, cleaner water, and cleaner soil since these things will be deemed necessary for the health of our people even if they are not profitable to this or that individual's "bottom line." With the Racial State, our young people will grow up feeling a great sense of belonging, purpose, and pride rather than the sense of alienation and disaffection with which they are currently burdened. With the Racial State, all of our White people will realize that they are the elite of the world, of value by virtue of their racial identity, their dedication to it, and their works for it. With the Racial State, our race survives and thrives. While men are able to conceive of other goals in this world, we lovers of White Life deem the goal of White people surviving and thriving to be of at *least* equal value to the best of them.

Hence we move towards the Racial State regardless of the obstacles of convention, of perceived impracticability, of governmental disdain, or worse. We move towards the Racial State if we wish to secure the existence of our small minority of White people upon the face of this planet. Submerged indefinitely by the other races, we are doomed. Only by separating ourselves can we live. We have witnessed the utter degradation of White culture in America, for example, when White people are still the *majority*, for goodness sakes. We have likewise witnessed the incidence of interracial breeding (genocide) multiply several times in only a few decades. We have experienced the fact that millions of White people have been raped, robbed, and murdered in societies where White people are supposedly *in charge*. How then can we be contented with our future when, as the demographers claim, we will no longer even be *in charge* anywhere on this earth if the present scheme of things continues? When we are a minority everywhere we live? The only solution is the advent of the Racial State where the only "majority" and "minority" will alike be composed of only our kind, where there will be no non-whites present anywhere to harm us, where power is totally *ours* for the benefit of *ourselves*. Power over our own destiny is not an evil but a good; rather it is the *lack* of power that is the evil. We have the choice before us then of a future that is bright and happy or one that is dark and miserable. We have the choice of *living* as a race or of continuing to *die* as a race and in fact acquiescing in that death. Only life is, and can be, the product of the Racial State; only death would be the consequence of the continued path of multiracialism. The past path doesn't have to be our destiny. We can break the chains of convention as much as we can break the chains of our mental slavery.

Racelessness can be replaced by racial consciousness; the integration of the races can be reversed. Our White people can band together and secure their place in the sun in this vast world.

About the Author

Reverend Matt Hale is the foremost religious prisoner of conscience in America today. From 1996 until his arrest in 2003, he led the World Church of the Creator, then the fastest growing pro-White organization in America. He was America's most well-known advocate for that cause, appearing numerous times on shows such as Today, Good Morning America, CBS This Morning, and others as well as being known for his public speeches around the country. A graduate of Southern Illinois University School of Law and an accomplished classical violinist, he was convicted in 2004 on phony charges of having solicited the murder of Federal District Court Judge Joan Lefkow even though there is no evidence that any such solicitation occurred. Nevertheless, this book is proof of the fact that his wrongful imprisonment has failed to stop him from fighting for our White people whom he loves. Now it is our task to place this book into as many hands of our people as possible. Do your part. His website is freematthale.net